BOUND FOR BATTLE
The Cruise of the U.S. Frigate Essex in the
War of 1812 as told by Captain David Porter
edited by Betty Shepard

"Following her success with another Essex
(THE WRECK OF THE WHALESHIP ESSEX), Betty
Shepard has condensed and edited to equally
good effect a second revealing eye-witness
account (and interpolated that of his adopted
son, then Midshipman David Farragut). The
Captain is as interesting as the cruise around
South America and into the Pacific: he showed
unusual insight in anticipating the psychologi-
cal and physical needs of his men and in de-
ploying and disguising the British ships he
captured; he was also a keen observer of par-
ticularities from the 'novelties' of a Chilean
ball to the strange habits of the Galapagos
turtle to the ingenious fortifications of the
Marquesas Indians. Abundantly laced with
action as well, efficiently bridged and thoroughly documented, this is rousing reading and
sound history."

Virginia Kirkus Service

"...The book is taken directly from Porter's
journals plus quotations from papers of other
people involved. The glossary is excellent
and the map helpful..."

School Library Journal

HARCOURT, BRACE & WORLD, INC.
757 Third Avenue, New York, N.Y.

BOUND FOR BATTLE

EDITED BY IOLA HAVERSTICK
AND BETTY SHEPARD

THE WRECK OF THE
WHALESHIP *ESSEX*

*A Narrative Account
by Owen Chase, First Mate*

Bound for Battle

The Cruise of the
United States Frigate ESSEX
in the War of 1812
as told by
Captain David Porter

EDITED, WITH INTRODUCTION
AND EPILOGUE, BY
Betty Shepard

ILLUSTRATED WITH
REPRODUCTIONS OF PRINTS
AND A MAP

HARCOURT, BRACE & WORLD, INC.
NEW YORK

For Paul, Reese, and Teddy

Several years ago in the course of a conversation with a friend about sea stories, the friend volunteered that Admiral Farragut had rounded the Horn as a midshipman in the War of 1812 and that this was a remarkable story. That friend was Mr. Laurie Y. Erskine, author of *Renfrew of the Royal Mounted*. In the course of checking into this information, I came across the journals of Captain David Porter and have been grateful to Mr. Erskine ever since. I am also grateful to Mr. William S. Cargill, whose enthusiasm over Captain Porter and Midshipman Farragut encouraged me to tackle the problem of editing Porter's rather lengthy account of that cruise.

This edition is considerably shorter than Captain Porter's *Journal of a Cruise Made to the Pacific Ocean*. Cuts have been made in those parts that did not materially affect the story; Captain Porter's original language has been left intact, with only minor changes for the sake of clarity. Some corrections in spelling have been made, and there have been various changes in punctuation. In addition, material from the journals of David Glasgow Farragut, written some thirty-five years later, has been included. An introduction has been added, as well as an epilogue giving the aftermath of the battle and what happened later to the *Essex,* her captain, and her crew.

The basis of this book is the second and last edition of Captain Porter's journals, published in 1822 by Wiley and Halsted of New York. Midshipman Farragut's sections were taken from *The Life of David Glasgow Farragut, Embodying His Journal and Letters,* written by his son Loyall Farragut and published in 1879 by D. Appleton and Company.

All quotations in the introduction and epilogue are from the above two sources, with the following exceptions. In the introduction: the contemporary comments on Captain Porter are from *Thirty Years from Home,* by Samuel Leech, Boston, 1843. Commodore William Bainbridge's orders to Captain Porter are in the National Archives in Washington.

In the epilogue: the Chilean eyewitness account of the battle is from "First Contacts—The Glorious Cruise of the Frigate *Essex,*" by Captain A. S. Merrill, *United States Naval Institute Proceedings,* February, 1940. It is reprinted from *Proceedings* by permission; copyright © 1949 U.S. Naval Institute. Captain Porter's memorandum to Lieutenant Downes is from "The First Cruise of the U.S. Frigate *Essex,*" by George Henry Preble, Essex Institute Historical Collections, Vol. 10, Salem, 1870. Porter's call to his crew is from *Memoir of Captain David Porter,* by his son Admiral David D. Porter, J. Munsell, Albany, 1875.

For background material and information in the introduction and epilogue, I have relied heavily on *David Glasgow Farragut, Admiral in the Making,* by Charles Lee Lewis, United States Naval Institute, 1941; and *The Age of Fighting Sail,* by C. S. Forester, Doubleday, New York, 1956.

I would like to express my appreciation to the following persons and institutions for their assistance: Mr. Stanley Crane and the Pequot Library in Southport, Connecticut; the Sterling Memorial Library at Yale University; Captain F. Kent Loomis, Mr. Henry A. Vadnais, Jr., Lieutenant (j.g.) Jeffrey D. Bogart, all of the Naval History Division, Department of the Navy, Washington; Mr. Richard A. von Doenhoff, Naval History, and Mr. Harry Schwartz, Old Military Records Division, both at the National Archives in Washington; Captain Dale Mayberry, the Museum, United States Naval Academy, Annapolis; Professor Vernon D. Tate, Naval Institute Library, and Mr. Tom Boone, Library Annex, both in Annapolis; Manuscript Division of the Library of Congress, Washington; Mr. Philip Chadwick Foster Smith, Maritime History, Peabody Museum in Salem, Massachusetts; Mr. Paul R. Tobey of the Boston Navy Yard; and Mr. B. Joseph O'Neil of the Boston Public Library.

Betty Shepard
January, 1967

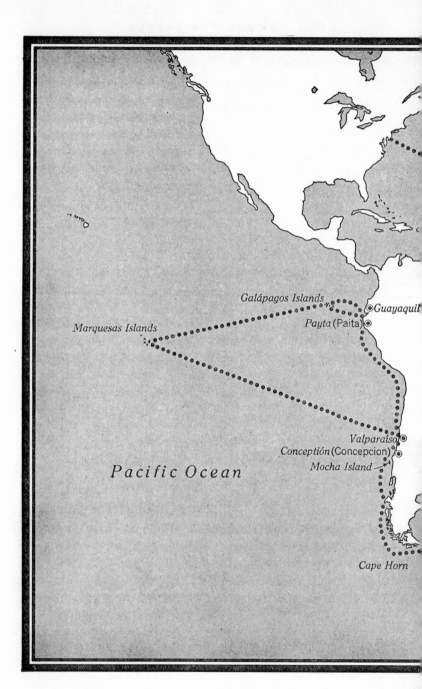

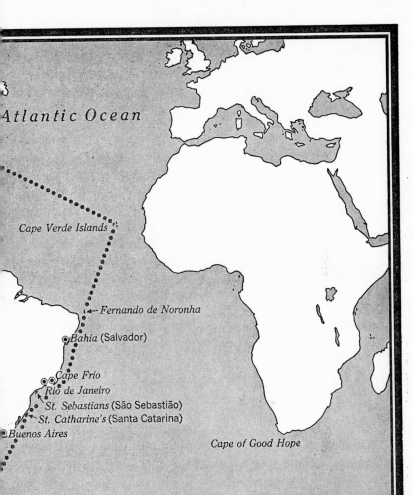

Atlantic Ocean

Cape Verde Islands

Fernando de Noronha

Bahia (Salvador)

Cape Frio
Rio de Janeiro
St. Sebastians (São Sebastião)
St. Catharine's (Santa Catarina)
Buenos Aires

Cape of Good Hope

The Cruise of the Essex

Oct. 28, 1812 - Mar. 28, 1814

Introduction

"I NEVER SAW AN OLD ESSEX WHO WAS NOT
THE BEST SHOT AND SWORDSMAN ABOARD HIS
SHIP."

Early in 1815, an account of an extraordinary sea voyage
by Captain David Porter, United States Navy, was published in Philadelphia. Entitled *Journal of a Cruise Made
to the Pacific Ocean,* it was soon vehemently attacked
by the Tory press of Great Britain and its author
compared unfavorably to Blackbeard and other notorious
pirates. What Captain Porter had done to deserve these
epithets was simply to fulfill his duties, as he saw them,
as a captain, during the War of 1812, in command of
the United States frigate *Essex.* His cruise started four
months after the outbreak of hostilities with England and
lasted until his capture in 1814. Sailing with him was
his adopted son, young Midshipman David Glasgow
Farragut.

When Congress declared war on Great Britain on June
18, 1812, that war was, in a sense, a continuation of
America's struggle for independence from Great Britain.

It was the logical reaction of a young nation that had been bullied and pushed around on the seas for twenty-five years by the most powerful of nations, traditional ruler of the waves.

In a message to Congress on June 1, President James Madison had stated the grievances of the United States against Great Britain. First and foremost was the practice of impressing American seamen and forcing them to serve on British ships of war. This practice had been a troublesome one for many years and was particularly so in the early 1800's, when Great Britain was intermittently at war with almost every other nation of Europe. The next grievance, English ships' violation of the sovereignty of American waters, was closely allied to England's claim that she could search neutral vessels, wherever found, for seamen.

Perhaps the most flagrant case of impressment had occurred in 1807 when the British ship *Leopard* fired on the United States Navy frigate *Chesapeake* and, when she surrendered, seized four of her crew as deserters. The situation became so serious that two years prior to the declaration of war, the American government published the figures on such impressments since 1803. The number was over four thousand men.

An additional grievance was the British Orders in Council, which blockaded the continent of Europe and forbade American trade with any country from which the British flag was excluded. American trade with other parts of Europe was to be permitted only on condition that the merchant vessels stop in England and pay duty.

So, the war aims of the United States, very specifically, were to put an end to British interference with American seamen, trade, and shipping. It was a fight for a free sea, and its slogan, "Free trade and sailors' rights," was the one Captain David Porter flew so proudly from the mast of the *Essex*.

When war came, the Navy, long a stepchild in the national economy, was passed over by the American cabinet in favor of a land offensive. It was decided that only privateering would be encouraged at sea and that the few available naval ships would be dismasted and used for harbor defense. Fortunately, Mr. Madison was persuaded by Commodore William Bainbridge, for one, to countermand this order. At that time a small squadron commanded by Commodore John Rodgers was in the New York harbor. It was the chief strength of the United States' small Navy and consisted of the two large frigates *President* and *United States*, the smaller frigate *Congress*, the frigate *Essex*, which was undergoing repairs, the sloop *Hornet*, and the brig *Argus*. Three days after the declaration of war, Rodgers, without waiting for orders, sailed with all but the *Essex* to sweep the North Atlantic.

On July 3 all was in order with the frigate *Essex*, which had been refitted with a new foremast, and she left port. Captain Porter, then thirty-two years old, had been promoted to the rank of captain the day before, and two days later Midshipman Farragut celebrated his eleventh birthday on board. After taking eight prizes in the next few weeks without any fighting, the frigate captured His Britannic Majesty's sloop *Alert*, of twenty guns, on the thirteenth of August. The *Alert*, taken in a brief skirmish of only eight minutes, was the first British man-of-war to be captured in the War of 1812. Only a few days after the *Alert* hauled down her colors, Captain Isaac Hull, who had sailed from Chesapeake Bay in July on the frigate *Constitution*, captured the British frigate *Guerriere*.

That autumn the United States fleet was divided into three squadrons, and Commodore Bainbridge fell heir to the command of the *Constitution*. Bainbridge's squadron was to be composed of the sloop *Hornet,* under the command of James Lawrence, and the *Essex.* The Commodore planned to sail after British commerce in the mid-Atlantic sometime in October. The *Essex,* meantime, needed refitting again and was moored in the Delaware River. Having notified Captain Porter by letter of their place of rendezvous, Bainbridge sailed from Boston on the *Constitution,* in company with the *Hornet,* on October 26. Porter sailed two days later from the Delaware.

Bainbridge never kept his rendezvous with Porter. In wartime it was unwise to wait weeks, or even days, to keep an appointment when the success of a raiding cruise depended on secrecy and the mobility of the ship. Instead, he left coded messages at various ports for the captain of the *Essex.*

In the meantime, the *United States,* under Commodore Stephen Decatur, captured the British frigate *Macedonian;* and the sloop of war *Wasp,* which had been in a French port at the time of the declaration of war, captured His Majesty's brig *Frolic.* Bainbridge celebrated Christmas that year off Bahia, where he left Lawrence and the *Hornet* to watch the British sloop of war *Bonne Citoyenne* while he cruised off shore in the *Constitution.* Porter, in the same waters at approximately the same time, had surmised that Commodore Bainbridge was either watching or chasing the *Bonne Citoyenne.* In late December the *Constitution* took the British frigate *Java* and returned home. Two months later the *Hornet* was also on her way home, having overcome and sunk His Majesty's brig *Peacock.*

At the beginning of the war, the United States Navy

had fewer than twenty ships and Great Britain more than eight hundred men-of-war. Supposedly, the American Navy was no adversary for the British, and yet, less than a year after the outbreak of hostilities, that same small fleet had won six actions in a row against the British. The Americans excelled in ship-to-ship combat, and it was quite apparent that in the art of gunnery they were also far superior.

There was another reason for the successes of the American Navy, however, and it had to do with qualities of leadership. Rodgers had had his command for two years prior to the war, and he had handled his men and drilled his crews well, giving them a sense of the importance of the United States Navy. Furthermore, the commanding officers were almost all young men with a high degree of confidence and individuality. Rodgers and Hull both took to sea as soon as possible after the declaration of war for fear the administration would keep them in port. Bainbridge helped talk President Madison out of his idea of making the Navy over into "floating batteries" and sailed immediately, before the administration could change its mind. Decatur was only thirty-three that fall, and he had already had command of the *United States* for two years.

Such a man, too, was Captain David Porter. His father had commanded a privateer during the Revolution. In 1796, at the age of sixteen, David went to sea with his father and got his first taste of fighting when they encountered a British man-of-war in Haitian waters. He entered the Navy two years later as a midshipman and was on board the *Constellation* when she captured the *Insurgente,* in the main frigate action of a brief naval war with France, in 1798. In the war with Tripoli a few years later, he served on board the *Enterprise,* was captured, and endured a long imprisonment. By 1806 Porter had been promoted to the rank of master commandant and soon after was in command of the New Orleans naval station. He held the post for several years before assuming command of the *Essex*.

Captain Porter's talents and his flamboyant personality are evident on every page of the journal that follows— his self-assurance in handling his crew, his prisoners, and the natives of the Marquesas, his knowledge of navigation and seamanship, his skill as the commander of a ship of war, his strategic judgment, and his courage.

One contemporary who served under Porter aboard the *Essex* said of him: "Although Captain Porter was stern and severe, he never used bad language. He always spoke with the utmost deliberation, but with such obvious indication of feeling that we often trembled to hear his voice." Later, a fellow captain, speaking of the way in which Porter trained his crews, remarked: "I never saw an old Essex who was not the best shot and swordsman aboard his ship."

For Midshipman Farragut, Porter was "all that he promised, a friend, a protector." The youth's relationship with his future captain began in 1808 under rather tragic circumstances. David Porter, Senior, and George Farragut, father of David G. Farragut, were sailing masters at the port of New Orleans and good friends, as well. The elder Porter fell suddenly ill and was taken into the Farragut home, where he died—of consumption, it is said —on June 22, 1808. That same day Mrs. Farragut died of yellow fever. David Porter, Junior, had just been ordered by the Department of the Navy to take command of the naval station, and he had arrived in New Orleans only five days earlier, bringing with him his young wife. Wishing to make some return for the Farraguts' kindness toward his father, he offered to take one of the Farragut children into his home and care for him. Young David went to live with Porter and was treated as a son, although there is no evidence that he was ever legally adopted.

In June of 1810, David Farragut was entirely separated from his own family when he accompanied the Porters from New Orleans to Washington. Within the next year, when he was barely ten years old, young Farragut received his appointment as a midshipman in the United States Navy, and Porter was ordered to take command of the frigate *Essex*. Porter took young David with him when he joined the frigate in August of 1811.

The life of a midshipman on a frigate during the War of 1812 was not an easy one. All the midshipmen, and there were twelve aboard the *Essex,* lived together in the steerage, or gun room, a section of the berth-deck across from the wardroom. For warmth in cold weather, they buried hot twenty-four-pound shot in buckets of sand. At sea they subsisted with the rest of the crew on hardtack, often infested with weevils, and jerked and salted beef. They also received a regular grog ration.

Early naval regulations state, "No particular duties can be assigned to this class of officers," but add, "They are promptly and faithfully to execute all the orders for the public service of their commanding officers."

Because of their youth, midshipmen were to be given "fostering care" by the officers and were to be instructed in the sciences and writing. Farragut, writing in his journal some thirty-five years later, tells of his indignation at being kept from fighting with the native tribes. He relates, also, that when the *Essex* arrived at the Marquesas, ". . . that evening I was sent on board the parson's ship to keep me out of the way of temptation, as the women were allowed to go on board the *Essex* to the number of four hundred." It was among the duties of the parson, apparently, to tutor the young midshipmen on the cruise.

The ship on which Farragut sailed and which Captain Porter commanded was an honorable one. She was built by Enos Briggs of Salem, Massachusetts, on a design prepared by William Hackett, leading ship designer of New England. The timbers for the ship's hull were cut in nearby wooded areas and hauled through Salem on sleds. The keel of the frigate was laid in April of 1799, and she was launched the following September. Her cordage was made in local ropewalks, her iron forged by Salem shipsmiths, and her sails cut from duck woven specifically for the purpose at a factory in town. Foremasts and mizzenmasts were fitted out at adjacent factories at the foot of Salem common. When her cables were completed, workmen placed them on their shoulders and marched to the ship, headed by a drum and fife. She was somewhat like the Revolutionary War frigates in appearance, but with guns on her forecastle. Hundreds of people visited the ship while she was building. At her launching, the guns of the frigate were placed on a nearby hill, where they fired a salute. The salute was returned by an armed vessel in the harbor. The *Essex*'s original battery consisted of twenty-six 12-pounders on her gun decks and ten 6-pounders on the quarter-deck, making thirty-six guns in all.

The *Essex*'s first captain was Captain Edward Preble, who sailed in December, 1799, for the island of Java to escort home a fleet of American merchantmen. During this maiden voyage the frigate became the first ship of war to double the Cape of Good Hope—just as, thirteen years later, under Captain Porter's command, she became the first American ship of war to round Cape Horn and carry the war into the Pacific.

She was originally a fast frigate, but changes made by her various commanders and by navy-yard commandants had slowed her sailing speed. By the time Porter took command, the *Essex* carried twenty-four 32-pound carronades and two long 12-pounders on the main gundeck, and sixteen 32-pounders and four long 12-pounders on the spar deck, making a total of forty-six guns. Porter objected to the Secretary of the Navy over the predominance of the carronades, but in vain.

In early October of 1812, Commodore William Bainbridge, aboard the United States frigate *Constitution* in the port of Boston, wrote the following orders to Captain David Porter:

"Sir. I shall sail from this port by the 25th instant and shall shape my course in the most direct way for the Cape Verde Islands where I shall stop at Port Praya [Praia] to fill up my water, and presume I shall leave there at furthest by the 27th November and hope I shall meet you there.

"From Port Praya Bay I shall proceed to the island Fernando de Noronha, at which place I shall get refreshments, and expect to leave there by the 15th December, thence cruise along the Brazil coast as far south as Cape Frio until the 15th January, at which time I intend to pass by Janeiro and cruise between that place and the island St. Sebastian [São Sebastião] until the 1st of February, when I shall stop at said island (Sebastian) to receive some refreshments, and shall leave it on the 3rd February and proceed to the island St. Catharine's [Santa Catarina], which place I shall leave by the 15th February.

"I shall then proceed off the island St. Helena and cruise to the southward of it, occasionally so near as to discover it. In this station I intend to remain to intercept the returning ships from India until the 1st of April.

"Should any unforeseen cause or accident prevent our meeting by the 1st of April next, you must act, according to your best judgment, for the good of the service in which we are engaged. I shall be extremely anxious for us to meet to communicate more fully and for me to receive your able assistance in advice and cooperation. With best wishes for the health and success of yourself, officers, and crew.

"I am, with sincere esteem and respect,
　　　"Your obedient servant,
　　　　William Bainbridge."

"THE SHIP BORE NO SLIGHT RESEMBLANCE . . . TO NOAH'S ARK."

October 6, 1812. I received orders from Commodore William Bainbridge to prepare the *Essex* for a long cruise, appointing places of rendezvous, and a copy of his orders from the honorable Secretary of the Navy.

I directed the ship to be furnished with every requisite supply of stores, ordered for her a new suit of sails and standing rigging, took out the bowsprit and fished it, and put her in the best possible state for service. I took in as much provision as she could stow and provided ourselves with a double supply of clothing and fruit, vegetables, and lime juice as antiscorbutics. I also gave the officers and men intimation of the probable length of our cruise and advanced the officers three months' pay.

On the afternoon of the 28th, we left the capes of Delaware with the wind from the northward. Prior to the pilot's leaving us, I caused him to deliver into my possession all letters which might have been given him by the crew, apprehensive that they might have become possessed of a knowledge of our destination. They all contained only conjectures except one, which stated that we were bound on the coast of Africa. As some of their conjectures were not far from being correct, I thought it best to destroy the whole of them and forbid the pilot's taking any more without my consent. To the officers who were desirous of writing to their friends, I enjoined particularly not to mention the movements of the ship in any way.

The wind gradually hauled around to the westward, blowing fresh with thick weather, so that it was with difficulty we were enabled to weather the dangerous shoals of Chincoteague. On the morning of the 29th, the wind increased to a gale. Got the ship under snug sail and secured our masts by setting up the rigging, which, being new, had stretched considerable.

Previous to leaving the river, the crew had been put on allowance of half a gallon of water each man per day. Having views with regard to the health of the crew, I caused the allowance of bread to be reduced one half and issued in lieu of the remainder half a pound of potatoes or the same quantity of apples. Every other article of provisions was reduced one third excepting rum, of which the full allowance was served out raw to the cook of each mess—the crew being divided into messes of eight and a cook allowed to each. For the undrawn provisions, the purser's steward was directed to issue due bills, with assurances on my part that they should be paid the amount on our arrival in port. Orders were given to lose no opportunity of catching rainwater for the stock, of which we had a large quantity on board, every mess in the ship being supplied with pigs and poultry.

I gave a general pardon for all offenses committed on board, recommended the strictest attention to the discipline of the ship, and held out prospects of reward to those who should be vigilant in the performance of their duty. I gave assurances that the first man I was under the necessity of punishing should receive three dozen lashes; expressing a hope, however, that punishment during the cruise would be altogether unnecessary.

I directed, as a standing regulation, that the ship should be fumigated in every part every morning by pouring vinegar on a red-hot shot. Cleats were put up for slinging as many hammocks as possible on the gun-deck and orders given that no wet clothes or wet provisions should be permitted to remain on the berth-deck, nor the crew be permitted to eat anywhere but on the gun-deck, except in bad weather. I exhorted the officers to keep the crew occupied during working hours in some useful employment and directed that two hours, between four and six o'clock in the afternoon, should be allowed to them for amusement when the duties of the ship would admit.

My crew at the time of my departure consisted of a total of 319 persons. There were on board: 1 captain, 5 lieutenants, 1 lieutenant of marines, 1 steward, 1 coxswain, 1 cooper, 1 sailing master, 1 chaplain, 1 purser, 1 surgeon, 2 surgeon's mates, 12 midshipmen, 1 boatswain, 1 gunner, 1 carpenter, 1 sailmaker, 2 master's mates, 1 captain's clerk, 3 boatswain's mates, 2 gunner's mates, 1 carpenter's mate, 1 armorer, 1 master-at-arms, 1 cook, 1 boatswain's yeoman, 1 gunner's yeoman, 1 carpenter's yeoman, 7 quartermasters, 7 quarter gunners, 2 sergeants,

2 corporals, 1 drummer, 1 fifer, 25 private marines, and 227 seamen, ordinary seamen, landsmen, boys, and supernumeraries.

I divided the crew into three watches, finding it sufficiently strong to admit of this arrangement, and took every advantage of the good weather to put the ship in prime order for any service.

On the 23rd of November, we were honored by a visit from the god of the ocean and a numerous retinue of imps and barbers. In the course of the afternoon, all the novices of the ship's company were initiated into his mysteries. Neptune, however, and most of his suite, paid their devotions so frequently to Bacchus that before the ceremony of christening was half gone through their godships were unable to stand. The business was therefore entrusted to the subordinate agents, who performed both the shaving and washing with as little regard to tenderness as his majesty would have done. On the whole, however, they got through the business with less disorder and more good humor than I expected. Although some were most unmercifully scraped, the only satisfaction sought was that of shaving others in their turn with new invented tortures.

At 2 P.M. on the 27th, we rounded to the east point of Port Praya [Praia], the first rendezvous fixed on by Commodore Bainbridge. We stretched into the harbor showing the American colors, the Portuguese being displayed on a flashy flagstaff erected on a hill at one corner of the ruins of a fort in front of the town.

Being desirous of procuring some information respecting the commodore, as this was the day appointed by him to leave this place for Fernando de Noronha, I sent Lieutenant Downes ashore. I directed him to state to the governor that we were an American frigate wanting supplies and to inform him I should fire a salute provided he would return gun for gun and that I should, provided I anchored, take the earliest opportunity of paying my respects to him. On his return Mr. Downes informed me that the governor could not be seen, as he had gone to take his afternoon nap, but that he would be happy to see me on shore. The lieutenant governor informed me we could obtain every supply we stood in need of.

Mr. Downes also ascertained that no government vessels of war had been at Praya; that an American privateer from Boston and another from Salem and an armed British schooner had been there not long since. I concluded on stopping a few days to fill up our water and take in refreshments. I ran in and anchored in seven fathoms' water, clear sandy bottom. We fired the salute, which was punctually returned.

The next morning I waited on his excellency, and his reception was of the most friendly nature. I informed him that, as the Portuguese were allies of Great Britain, I had entertained doubts whether he would feel authorized to give us protection against a superior British force should it appear. He expressed much regret that the war had deprived them of the advantages arising from American commerce, as they had been cut off from all their supplies and were destitute of bread and every other comfort of life except what the island afforded, which consisted chiefly in livestock and fruit. He told me that a little flour, or anything else that we could spare, would be most acceptable to him.

We this day commenced watering but, after having to roll the casks about 500 yards, found great difficulty in getting them from the beach on account of the heavy surf. We were only enabled to get about 5,000 gallons.

The beef was very dear and very poor. A bullock

weighing 300 weight cost $35. Sheep were $3, but very poor. Oranges cost 40 cents per 100, and other fruits in the same proportion and in the greatest abundance. The ship had on board not less than 100,000 oranges together with a large quantity of coconuts, plantains, lemons, limes, casaba. Every mess on board was also supplied with pigs, sheep, fowls, turkeys, goats, which were purchased tolerably cheap—fowls at $3 per dozen and fine turkeys at $1 each. Many of the seamen also furnished themselves with monkeys and young goats as pets, and when we sailed from thence, the ship bore no slight resemblance, as respected the different animals on board her, to Noah's ark.

There are not more than 30 whites in the town of Praya. The rest of the population is made up of slaves and free Negroes, making altogether not more than 3,000, of whom about 400 are soldiers. All the officers, except three or four, are mulattoes, and their priest is a Negro who possesses considerable polish of manners. The soldiers are generally destitute of clothing from the waist up, and there are not five serviceable muskets in Praya. It was no uncommon thing to see a naked Negro mounting guard, shouldering a musket barrel only. Their cavalry were in a corresponding style, mounted on jackasses and armed with broken swords. The governor informed me it had been ten years since they had received any pay or supplies of clothing or arms.

The guns of different calibers mounted about Praya for the defense of the place, although in commanding situations, are in a state equally bad with the muskets of the Negroes. They are placed on ships' carriages which are old and rotten, scarcely holding together, without platform, shelter, or breastwork. The whole number of guns amounts to 30, and for them chiefly they are indebted to a Portuguese frigate that was lost by the negligence of her officers about three years since. Port Praya could be taken, and every gun spiked, by 30 men.

An abundance of fish may be caught with the hook and line alongside, and with the seine on the beach, where we hauled every morning during our stay. A very good amusement may be had in the bay by rowing with a small boat across the mouth and towing a line with a hook fastened on with wire and baited with small fish for the purpose of catching barracudas. The best time is in the dusk of the evening and at daylight in the morning.

I found that the only British vessels that ever touched at Port Praya were vessels of war, who came for supplies with the haughty, unconciliating conduct of the commanders and officers. The people of Praya spoke of the Prince Regent as the slave, the tool of the British government, and were highly gratified with the accounts I gave them of our little success over the ships of the imperious Navy. The governor assured me he would give me every protection against any British force that should arrive here during my stay.

The two greatest evils to guard against in refreshing at Praya are the bad rum of the country and the heat of the sun, to both of which the watering party is unavoidably exposed. The Negroes and seamen have such a variety of expedients for getting rum on board that it is almost impossible to detect them. The inhabitants of the port hover about the beach with the bottles under their arms, where the shawls of the females serve the better to conceal them. At a favorable opportunity they bury them in the sand and receive their money, while the sailor watches his opportunity for getting it on board or drinking it. Sometimes the inhabitants draw the milk from coconuts, fill them with rum, and sell them to the seamen at a high price.

The first day we were employed in watering, we had several men drunk. After that I selected the most trusty men to fill and roll the casks to the beach, with directions to make a signal when they were ready to tow off. By this means we prevented our boats' crews from having any communication with the shore.

On leaving the port, we shaped our course to the southeast with a view to deceiving the people of Praya and impressing a belief that we were bound for the coast of Africa.

My chief care now was the health of my people. The utmost cleanliness was required from every person on board, and directions were given for mustering the crew every morning at their quarters, where they were strictly examined by their officers. It was recommended to them to bathe at least once a day, and the officers were requested to show them the example.

Economy was recommended to the crew in the use of their supply of fruit. Permission was given to suspend it in the rigging and other airy parts of the ship, in nets made for the purpose, with a promise of the severest punishment to such as should be detected in stealing from others.

Finding that the large quantity of stock on board must necessarily consume a great deal of water or suffer, I directed that the seamen should kill all their pigs. As the young goats, by sucking the old, deprived us of their milk, I directed that they also should be killed. Many petitions were sent in to me to save from slaughter a favorite kid, or a pig that was destined for a Christmas dinner, with assurances from the owner that it should be supplied with water from his own allowance, although each man was allowed only half a gallon. I found it necessary to be inflexible to avoid the imputation of partiality. If I had granted the petition in one instance, I should have had to do so in all, and the quantity of stock, and the dirt occasioned by them, were no inconsiderable inconvenience on board.

The regulation of permitting the crew to sleep on the gun-deck with the ports open, where they have a free circulation of air, contributes not a little, in my opinion, to the preservation of their health. Most commanders are averse to this indulgence, supposing the hammocks in the way of the guns. I find a great advantage in always having the men near their quarters, where, on the slightest alarm, they may be ready for action. Should circumstances make it necessary for us to pipe up the hammocks on seeing a strange sail at night, they can be lashed up much sooner and with less confusion on a roomy gundeck than from a dark and crowded berth-deck. If a vessel is close on board before she is discovered, it is an easy matter to cut away the lanyards and throw the hammocks below, or on one side, clear of the guns. None are permitted to sleep on the gun-deck but those who are quartered at the guns there; they sling the hammocks opposite their guns and are accountable for the safety of every article belonging to them.

What can be more dreadful than for 300 men to be confined, with their hammocks only 18 inches apart, on the berth-deck of a small frigate, a space of 70 feet long, 35 feet wide, and 5 feet high, in a hot climate, where the only apertures by which they can receive air are two hatchways of about 6 feet square? From the number confined in so small a space, the whole atmosphere of the ship becomes tainted, and not only those who are compelled to sleep below, but every person on board is affected by the pernicious vapors arising from the berth-deck.

Various expedients have been adopted to remove this foul air—fumigation with gunpowder and burning fires below, purifying by sprinkling vinegar, and ventilating by means of wind sails. But the most effectual remedy, although the most uncomfortable, is the French practice of baking bread in ovens built on the berth-deck. While the ovens are heating, a constant current of air rushes toward the fire, the foul air is carried off, and fresh air rushes in to supply its place.

About 2 P.M. on the 12th of December, discovered a sail to windward which bore the appearance of a British brig of war and made all sail in chase of her. With a view to decoying her down to me, I displayed such British signals as I became possessed of during my last cruise, but without effect.

When within musket shot I hailed her and directed her to lower her topsails, haul up her courses, and heave to, to windward. She attempted to run athwart my stern, with a view, as I supposed, to rake us and make her escape. I directed a volley of musketry to be fired, which, I am sorry to say, killed one man on board her.

She proved to be His Majesty's packet *Nocton,* bound to Falmouth, of 10 guns and 31 men. I that night took out the prisoners and a quantity of specie found on board, amounting to about $55,000. The next day I dispatched the prize. As I sent in her 17 of the prisoners, I was under the necessity of parting with as many of my own crew. I permitted the prisoners to go on parole of honor with the privilege of embarking on any vessel they might meet, bound to England or elsewhere.

The *Nocton* proving to be a beautiful vessel and well calculated for the United States service, I took the liberty of recommending her to the Secretary of the Navy as a cruiser. I was anxious that one of the enemy's small vessels should be taken into our service to supply the place of the *Nautilus*, which had been taken by the British a short time before.

On the afternoon of December 14th, made the high peak, called the Pyramid, of the island of Fernando de Noronha. At daylight the next day, bore up for the harbor, disguised the ship as a merchantman, hoisted English colors, ran close in, and sent the boat on shore with Lieutenant Downes in plain clothes. I directed him to inform the governor that we were the ship *Fanny*, Captain Johnson, from London via Newfoundland, bound to Rio de Janeiro for a cargo, out 60 days. He was to say we were short of water, had several of the crew sick with scurvy, and were very much in want of refreshments. Also, that we could not anchor, as we had lost all our anchors but one, and that our cables were bad.

After being absent two hours and a half, Lieutenant Downes informed me that two British frigates had left there the past week, that they had reported themselves to the governor as His Majesty's ships *Acasta*, Captain Kerr, of 44 guns, and the *Morgiana*, of 20 guns, from England bound to India. Also, that a letter had been left by the captain of the *Acasta* for Sir James Yeo of His Majesty's frigate *Southampton*, to be sent to England at the first opportunity. He also brought me a small present of fruit from the governor.

I immediately dispatched Lieutenant Downes with a

present of porter and cheese to the governor, with many thanks for his extreme civility, and to inform him that there was a gentleman on board who was intimately acquainted with Sir James Yeo and going from Brazil direct to England. He would take charge of the letter and deliver it to Sir James.

About three o'clock Lieutenant Downes returned with the letter, which I found to contain as follows:

"My dear Mediterranean friend,

"Probably you may stop here; don't attempt to water; it is attended with too much difficulty. I learnt before I left England that you were bound for the Brazil coast. If so, perhaps we may meet at St. Salvadore [Salvador] or Rio de Janeiro. I should be happy to meet and converse on our old affairs of captivity, recollect our secret in those times.

"Your friend of H. M. ship *Acasta*, Kerr."

The following was written in sympathetic ink.

"I am bound off St. Salvadore, thence off Cape Frio, where I intend to cruise until the 1st of January. Go off Cape Frio, to the northward of Rio de Janeiro, and keep a lookout for me."

As this was the second rendezvous fixed on by Commodore Bainbridge, I was not at a loss to divine whence the letter was from, nor for whom it was intended. We immediately hoisted up our boat and made sail to the southward.

On the 20th, spoke a Portuguese vessel from St. Salvadore, out 18 days. We boarded her under English colors, and on the captain's coming on board, he informed me that an English sloop of war had put into St. Salvadore in distress a short time before. From the description he gave me of this vessel, there could be no doubt of her being His Majesty's sloop of war the *Bonne Citoyenne,* of which we obtained intelligence by the *Nocton.* She had sailed six days before the *Nocton* and was so deep as to be thought by many very unsafe. The Portuguese informed me that she had sprung a leak from having been on shore, had taken out all her guns and money, and was preparing to heave out.

My first intention was to go and cruise off St. Salvadore until she came out, and I made all sail for that port. But on a little reflection, I thought it not unlikely that Commodore Bainbridge would, on arriving off St. Salvadore, continue to cruise there for the *Bonne Citoyenne.* If so, my presence there would prove unnecessary. I concluded it incumbent in me to be punctual to the time and place of every rendezvous and made the best of my way for Cape Frio, whence I should proceed to St. Sebastians [São Sebastião], if it should be advisable to do so.

The land we first discovered was high and irregular, and I had every reason to believe it to be part of a group of islands to the north of Cape Frio. I therefore hauled to the southward to make the Cape, ran down, and hove to off the pitch of it to meet the arrival of vessels bound to Rio de Janeiro, this being the point they endeavor to make from the north as well as south. It is considered as eligible a place as any in those seas for cruising against the enemy's commerce.

On the morning of the 29th, the man at the masthead descried a sail to windward. On going into the maintop with my glass, I perceived she was a schooner and standing in for the harbor of Rio. Made all sail in chase to endeavor to cut her off, but did not succeed in bringing her to until about nine o'clock at night, when, after our firing several shot at her, she bore up and ran under our lee.

She proved to be the British schooner *Elizabeth*, from Rio bound to England, but had put back in consequence of having sprung a leak. After taking the prisoners out, we discovered that she had parted with a convoy of British vessels under charge of the *Juniper*, a three-masted schooner, about half an hour before she was discovered by us. The *Juniper* had sailed the night before from Rio with 6 vessels in company—a cutter, 4 ships, and the *Elizabeth*. The cutter had gone to the southward to convoy a ship to St. Sebastians, and the *Juniper* had proceeded to the eastward with the three others, which were deeply laden and dull-sailing ships.

I also obtained certain intelligence that the British admiral's ship the *Montague* was still at Rio de Janeiro with all her sails unbent; that a packet had sailed for England on Christmas Day; and that there were no British vessels there expected to sail shortly. Believing that I should be enabled to overtake the convoy in a few days by carrying a press of sail, I used every exertion to get clear of the schooner *Elizabeth*.

On the 2nd of January, discovered two sail to windward and gave chase to one, which bore the appearance of a brig of war. She proved to be a Portuguese brig of war, nine days from Bahia [Salvador], where she left the *Bonne Citoyenne*. She had been boarded, the day after she came out, by a frigate mounting 50 guns, having a sloop of war in company, under English colors.

Knowing that the enemy had but three ships of war in those seas—the *Montague* of 74, the *Nerus* of 32, and the *Bonne Citoyenne* of 20 guns (the first at Rio de

Janeiro, the second at the River of Plate [La Plata], and the third at Bahia)—I was very well satisfied that the frigate and sloop of war could be no others than the American frigate *Constitution* and the sloop of war *Hornet*. As I expected that they would remain there to endeavor to take the *Bonne Citoyenne,* I determined to join them with all dispatch.

I requested the commander of the brig to call on the admiral immediately on his arrival at Rio de Janeiro and to inform him that he had spoken His Majesty's frigate *Hyperion,* of 32 guns, seven weeks from England, bound to Rio. Also, to inform him that having heard of a large American privateer on the coast, I intended staying to cruise for her for a short time before I went in. He promised me he would make it his business to do so immediately on his arrival.

My motive for giving this information was to keep the admiral in port, as I had certain intelligence from the prisoners that he expected reinforcements from England. I was in hopes that the expectation of their arrival in a few days might occasion him to delay his departure in pursuit of the ships off Bahia. This would enable me to cruise more leisurely for the convoy and give sufficient time to join the commodore before the admiral could get there, as I believed that the *Constitution, Essex,* and *Hornet* would be a match for him.

Since I left the United States, the crew had been on two thirds' allowance of salt provisions, generally on half allowance of bread and full allowance of rum. Every month I caused them to be paid the amount due them for undrawn rations. To this regulation they submitted cheerfully; not a murmur was heard from any person on board. I, however, found it necessary to reduce the allowance of rum in the same proportion as the salt provisions, when every man in the ship refused to receive any of that precious liquor unless he could get full allowance—stating that when there would be no more on board, they would willingly go without, but so long as it lasted, they wished their full allowance.

As there was but a small quantity in the ship, and believing that a sudden privation of it altogether would cause sickness and dejection among them, I determined not to indulge their wishes. I therefore directed the grog-tub to be upset in 15 minutes after they were called to grog. The consequence was that every man hastened to the tub for fear of losing his allowance. After this, no further complaint was made.

Since leaving Port Praya we had no opportunity of procuring refreshments. Our water was getting short, and it became necessary to ascertain what prospect we had of a supply of salt provisions, bread, and rum. I therefore determined to proceed to the island of St. Catharine's [Santa Catarina], and with a view of enabling the officers and crew to provide themselves with such articles as they might need, I distributed among them a large proportion of the prize money taken from the *Nocton.* Giving it to the seamen before they had an opportunity of spending it (although it had the effect of producing cheerfulness among them) was attended with evil consequences, as it introduced gambling and was the cause of some thefts. I soon put a stop to it by signifying that he who asked for, or paid, a gambling debt should be punished and that all moneys staked in gambling should be forfeited to the informer, whose name should remain secret.

At St. Catharine's I had not much to apprehend from an attack, as I had understood the place was well fortified and could protect us. Added to this, it was a place of importance. I should be enabled to procure a supply of bread, flour, rum, and many other articles of provisions and stores, which would enable me to meet at the last appointed rendezvous.

Commodore Bainbridge had appointed to meet me at Praya, Fernando de Noronha, and at Cape Frio. St. Sebastians was the fourth place appointed, but as he had changed his whole plan of remaining off Bahia, I thought it just as likely that he would touch first at St. Catharine's, the fifth place of rendezvous.

"THE BLACK CLOUDS HANGING OVER CAPE HORN BURST UPON US WITH A FURY WE LITTLE EXPECTED."

On the 19th of January, made the island of St. Catharine's. Immediately on anchoring, I dispatched a boat with Lieutenant Downes to inform the commander of the fort that we were Americans and in want of supplies, and to come to an understanding about a salute. He returned in about two hours with offers of civilities and a promise from the commander that he would send a pilot on board to take the ship nearer in.

About nine o'clock in the morning, an officer came on board with the pilot, and we got under way with a light baffling wind from the southward and the tide in our favor, which generally runs here about one and a half knots. After our making two tacks, the wind and the tide both failed us. We were then about two miles from the place I wished to anchor in.

Being anxious to get the vessel secured as soon as possible, and finding that our boats could give us very little assistance in towing, I put in operation an invention of mine for propelling a ship in a calm. In three quarters of an hour, we were at anchor at the back of the fort and opposite the most convenient watering place. The contrivance consists of two floating anchors, six feet square, which are worked on both sides of the ship by hauling lines from the spritsail yard and a spar rigged across the stern. The line from the spritsail yard is made fast to the upper corner of the anchor. When hauled on, it brings the anchor forward, skimming along on the surface of the water. When let go, the anchor falls, by means of the weight attached to it, in a vertical position. As it is slung something in the manner of a log-chip, and the rope to the stern made fast to the spar, it is dragged aft, propelling the ship in proportion to the force applied to the drag rope. A ship's crew, consisting of 300 men, will drag her forward in a calm with this contrivance at the rate of two miles an hour.

In two days and a half, we completed watering our ship and got as much wood on board as we had consumed since our departure from the United States. The officers and men, in the meantime, provided themselves with hogs, fowls, plantains, yams, and onions in considerable quantities from the boats alongside.

The Portuguese asked the most extravagant prices for everything, which some of our people had the folly to give, as if their stock of money was inexhaustible. This made my interference necessary. I first began by punishing a man for paying a dollar for a dozen rotten eggs. Next, I would not permit the boats to sell, after they had come alongside, until the price of every article was established as follows: three fowls, one dollar; nine watermelons for the same sum; one dollar for a turkey, and everything else in the same ratio. By this means I brought the market down to tolerably fair rates.

I waited on the commander of the fort the day after I anchored. He was a very old man, and he received me with great civility. At the entrance of the commandant's apartments are the stocks for the punishment of the soldiers. I have reason to believe they are kept in constant use, from their greasy, polished appearance.

About one and a half leagues below the fortress, behind a rocky point going into the bay, are the houses for the accomodation of those employed in the whale fishery, as well as the stóres, boilers, and tanks to contain the oil. The crown has the exclusive privilege of fishing here. About 500 men are engaged in it. Nearly the same number of whales are taken annually in the bay, where they come to calve and are then perfectly helpless. None but small boats are engaged in taking them. The oil is deposited in an immense tank, formed for the purpose in a rock, and is from thence transported to Portugal and elsewhere.

I went to this bay to procure a quantity of jerked beef for the use of the crew, having heard of the arrival of a vessel with a cargo. On my way, I met a small vessel four days from Rio de Janeio and went on board to learn the news. The captain informed me that two days before he sailed, an American corvette had arrived there, a prize to the *Montague*. She had been in company with a large frigate and was captured off the Albrothas shoal. He also informed me that the day before he sailed, a British frigate and two brigs of war had arrived from England and that two American schooners had been captured and sent in there. Also, that a Portuguese brig of war had arrived from the Cape of Good Hope and brought intelligence that a British 60-gun ship was to sail the day after her for Rio de Janeiro, and that several ships of war were daily expected from England.

Feeling confident that the captured vessel was the *Hornet,* and having strong apprehensions of being blockaded, if not attacked, by a superior force in this port, I determined on getting to sea again with all possible expedition. I therefore returned to the ship, made a signal for every person to repair on board, hove up, and dropped down below the fort.

We were clear of the island about four o'clock on the morning of the 26th. It was then necessary to decide promptly on my future proceedings, as our provisions were getting short. I called on the purser for a report and found that we had but three months' bread at half allowance. There was no port on this coast where we could procure a supply without the certainty of capture or blockade. To attempt to return to the United States at a season of the year when our coast would be swarming with the enemy's cruisers would be running too much risk. I was perfectly at a loss now where to find the commodore, as he had departed from his original intentions and had already disappointed me at three rendezvous. The state of my provisions would not admit of going off to St. Helena's to intercept returning Indiamen, nor would my force justify the proceeding.

I therefore determined to pursue that course which seemed best calculated to injure the enemy and would enable me to prolong my cruise. This could only be done by going into a friendly port where I could increase my supplies without the danger of blockade. The first place that presented itself to my mind was the port of Conception [Concepción], on the coast of Chili [Chile].

The season, to be sure, was far advanced for doubling

Cape Horn, but there appeared no other choice left for me except capture, starvation, or blockade. This course appeared the most justifiable, as it accorded with the views of my superiors. Before the declaration of war, I wrote letters to the Secretary of the Navy and to Commodore Bainbridge, containing a plan for annoying the enemy's commerce in the Pacific Ocean, which was approved of by both men.

My stock of provisions, agreeable to the purser's report, was as follows: 184 barrels of beef, 114 barrels of pork, 21,763 pounds of bread, 1,741 gallons of spirits, 201 gallons of vinegar, 108 gallons of molasses, 10 boxes of spermaceti and 17 of tallow candles. On two thirds allowance of beef and half allowance of bread, other articles in the same proportion as the beef, there was sufficient to serve us as follows: beef, 36 weeks and 5 days; pork, 22 weeks and 5 days; bread, 22 weeks and 1 day; spirits, 13 weeks and 2 days; vinegar, 6 weeks and 4 days; molasses, 7 weeks and 5 days.

I estimated it would not take me more than two months and a half to get round to Conception, where I was confident of procuring an abundant supply of jerked beef, fish, flour, and wine. I calculated that the prizes we should make in the Pacific would supply us with such articles of naval stores as we should require. Immediately on getting to sea, I directed my course to the southward.

Before leaving St. Catharine's, I wrote a letter to be delivered to the commander of any American frigate that should put into the port. The letter ran as follows:

"Your letter of the 3rd of December has been received. Yeo has been punctual. I have taken but two vessels. It is much to be regretted that we have not yet met. I have just heard of the capture of the *Hornet*. Should we not meet by the 1st of April, be assured that, by pursuing my own course, I shall have been actuated by views to the good of the service, and there will have been an absolute necessity for my doing so. As an American, I have been well treated here. I am afraid to trust more to this letter. January 20th, 1813."

St. Catharine's has been the usual stopping place for all American vessels engaged in the southern whale fishery, on their return to the United States. Four fishing vessels had left it for America about a month before I arrived, and they here received the first intelligence of the war.

The whole of the 26th of January, we had fresh gales from the southward, which I took advantage of to get a good offing. The weather continued fine and the wind fair until the 28th, when the wind freshened up so as to compel us to send down our royal yards and double-reef our topsails. The cold began now to be sensibly felt, and woolen clothing was more esteemed than it had been for some time past. The old jackets and trousers that had been lying about the ship were carefully collected, as some suspicions of my intention of doubling Cape Horn had got among the crew.

Believing that we should have but little use for our light sails until we doubled the Cape, I caused the sky-sails, royal studding sails, and such other sails as are only fit for tropical weather to be unbent and put below. I took measures to meet the worst by sending down our royal masts and rigging, unreeving all our running rigging not absolutely necessary, and sending every heavy article out of the tops. I also caused all the shot to be put below except six to each gun on the gun-deck, removed the guns from the extremities to midships, set up the main rigging, and bent the storm staysails. With a view to keeping the ship from straining as much as possible, I got all our spare spars from the spar to the gun-deck, and struck down two long 12-pounders from the forecastle.

In the course of our run after leaving St. Catharine's, we frequently discovered those yellow tracks in the ocean, extending several leagues and called by seamen the sperm of whales. (Whales have been known to disgorge large quantities of a yellow substance which floats on the surface of the water.) To me, it had the appearance of dirty oil, and the water did not appear colored more than two or three feet deep. All the tracks we met with were in a line with the coast, as far as the sight could reach. We frequently met three, and sometimes more, only a mile or two distant in lines parallel to each other. They seldom were more than the width of a ship, and have much the same appearance as shoals at first sight.

To guard against future wants, it now became necessary to economize in everything that related to the ship's stores. I gave orders that nothing whatever would be issued from the storerooms without my orders. And with a view of guarding against that dreadful scourge, the scurvy, I gave strictest orders to the cook not to permit any person to use the slush from the cask for the purpose of frying their bread. This practice is very common among seamen, and on many ships the disease has been traced to this cause. I made inquiries into the purser's slops and found we had but a small number of shoes. As every man in the ship was in want of a pair, I determined not to issue any until we arrived in a more southern latitude, so that I might judge who were most in want. I directed, however, one pair of woolen stockings to be issued to such as required them.

On February 13th the wind continued to increase and the weather became more hazy, with rain. At four o'clock, the appearance of a strong current, which was indicated by a violent ripple, and an unusual quantity of kelp, together with considerable flocks of birds resembling geese, induced me to believe I must be very near the shore. I therefore caused a good lookout to be kept, took in topgallant sails, double-reefed the topsails, furled the mainsail, and had everything prepared in case it should be necessary to haul our wind. At half past six, had cause to rejoice I had taken such precautions, as breakers were discovered distant about three fourths of a mile, and a few minutes afterward, land appeared in the same direction.

We hauled on a wind to the eastward and sounded in 45 fathoms' water. We had now approached so close to the breakers, with the hope of weathering them, that we had not room to wear. There was a tremendous sea running, the ship driving forecastle under, and the violence of the current was such that it was impossible for any man to stand without grasping something to support himself. Our only hope of safety was in getting the ship in stays. The mainsail was set with the utmost expedition, and, after we got the ship about, the jib and spanker were set and the topgallant yards sent down. In a few moments, the jib was blown to pieces. As the gale was increasing and night fast approaching, the thick weather continuing and the wind directly on shore, I saw no prospect of saving the ship but by carrying a heavy press of sail to keep off the lee shore until the wind changed.

After we stood to the west-northwest about an hour, the water began to grow very smooth, which could only be occasioned by a sudden change of the current. Whales appeared alongside the ship. This gave me the hope of being in the Straits of Le Maire. A sharp lookout was kept for the land, and at half past seven, to our unspeakable joy, land was discovered ahead and on both bows, distant about a mile. No doubts now remained as to our being in the straits. We undoubtedly had the first of the tide and were swept through with great rapidity. At nine o'clock we were clear of the straits.

On the meridian of the 14th, the horizon was somewhat clear, the wind moderate from the westward, the sun shining out bright, and, with the exception of some dark and lowering clouds to the northward, we had every prospect of pleasant weather. The Cape was now in sight. Of a sudden, the black clouds hanging over Cape Horn burst upon us with a fury we little expected and reduced us in a few minutes to a reefed foresail and close-reefed main topsail, and a few hours afterward, to our storm staysails. We, however, escaped any injury of importance except the loss of our spritsail yard, which was carried away by a heavy sea.

On the afternoon of the 18th, a gale came on from the westward. I determined to carry all the sail in my power to get to the northward as fast as possible and, with great difficulty, succeeded in getting the close-reefed main topsail set. With this and the fore, main, and mizzen storm staysails, we were enabled to force the ship about two knots through a tremendous head sea which threatened, every moment, destruction to our bowsprit and masts. The gale, however, increasing, we were soon reduced to the main storm staysail and from that to bare poles. At twelve o'clock the wind hauled around to the southwest and blew in dreadful squalls, accompanied with hail. The squalls came at intervals of from 15 to 20 minutes with so little warning and with such tremendous blasts that it was impossible to shorten sail; for to have started the sheets, after the squalls had struck the ship, would have been attended with the certain loss of the sail. I therefore saw no alternative but running before the wind while they lasted, and as soon as they were over, which was generally in two or three minutes, hauled again by the wind.

Thus, by the utmost attention and care, we were enabled to get along at the rate of between five and six miles per hour. We had now fair prospects of soon getting around. I had made large allowances for drift and leeway and believed ourselves as far to the west as our reckoning gave us, which I considered sufficient to take us clear of all land if the westerly winds should prevail. Having now no doubt of succeeding speedily in my passage to a friendly port where we could get supplies, I, to the great joy of all on board, ordered the allowance of bread to be increased to two thirds.

Although we deemed ourselves more fortunate than other navigators had been in getting around Cape Horn (for we considered our passage now as certain), yet we had not been without our share of hardships. The weather for some days had been piercing cold—this, with the almost constant rains and hails and the water shipped from heavy seas and from leaks, kept the vessel very uncomfortable and the clothes of the officers and crew uncomfortably wet. The extremities of those who had formerly been affected by the frost became excessively troublesome to them, so much so as to prevent some from doing their duty. From this cause I myself was a sufferer. Many, also, felt severely the great want of shoes and the necessary quantity of woolen clothing. Their allowance of provisions was barely sufficient to satisfy the cravings of nature. And as to refreshments of any kind, they were entirely out of the question, our scanty supply obtained at St. Catharine's having been long consumed. The fatigues of the officers and crew were very considerable, although I endeavored to alleviate them as much as possible by only keeping the watch on deck. The state of our ship necessitated that we make our passage as short as possible, and we were constantly harassed by making and taking in sail. To be sure, we had not much to take in, but what we had were heavy and required all hands to manage them.

With great industry and extraordinary good fortune, we had succeeded in getting, by our reckoning, as far to the westward as 77 degrees west longitude. But when an opportunity presented itself for taking a lunar observation, we discovered, to our great disappointment and regret, that we were only in the longitude of 75 degrees 20 points west. Great and mortifying as this discovery was to us, it was not to be overcome but by renewed efforts and fortitude. As the wind hauled around to the northward, it gave us a prospect of soon recovering our lost ground. I permitted the crew to continue to draw their increased allowance of bread. I did not wish them to feel the extent of my disappointment, which perhaps would have been attended with a depression of their spirits.

The crew, notwithstanding their constant labor, fatigue, and privations, enjoyed the most extraordinary spirits. They continued their usual diversions during the gales, labored with cheerfulness when labor was requisite, and all seemed determined to share with their officers every fatigue and to exert themselves to the utmost to conquer every difficulty. To be sure, we had not been long in these seas. But since we left America, they had been deprived of almost every comfort of life. So great was their desire now for fresh meat that a rat was esteemed a dainty, and pet monkeys were sacrificed to appease their longings.

Our provisions and water continued good. The bread had been attacked by worms and weevils, but they had only in a slight degree altered its qualities. Our peas and beans, however, had not escaped so well. As the allowance of water enabled us to spare enough to permit boiling them, I directed them to be served. On opening the barrels, we found only a mass of chaff and worms. The rats, also, had found the way into our bread rooms.

On February 24th I had the extreme satisfaction to find ourselves as far to the westward as 80 degrees. I increased the allowance of water in order that the crew might be enabled to spare enough to afford them tea morning and night. I was convinced this would conduce as much to their health as their comfort. I also took an opportunity of thanking them for their good conduct during our boisterous and unpleasant passage around the Cape. As some thefts had been committed for which the perpetrators were then under the punishment of wearing a yoke, I gave a general pardon on condition the first offender brought to the gangway should receive three dozen lashes.

It was with no little joy that we saw ourselves fairly in the Pacific Ocean and calculated on a speedy end to our suffering. We also began to form our projects for annoying the enemy and had already equipped, in imagination, one of their vessels of 14 or 16 guns, manned from the *Essex*, to cruise against their commerce. Indeed, various were the schemes we formed at this time for injuring them, and we had already, in fancy, immense wealth to return with to our country.

In the afternoon the wind hauled around to the westward and blew with a fury even exceeding anything we had yet experienced. From the succession of bad weather, our sails and standing and running rigging had become so damaged as to be no longer trustworthy. We took, however, the best means in our power to render everything secure and carried as heavy a press of sail as the ship would bear to keep her from drifting on the coast of Patagonia. We had reason to believe land was not far distant, from the clouds to leeward, which appeared as if arrested by the high mountains of the Andes. Our pumps had become choked by the shingle ballast, which had got into them from the violent rolling of the ship. The whole ocean was one continued foam of breakers, and the heaviest squall I ever before experienced did not equal in violence the most moderate intervals of this hurricane. We turned our attention to the pumps, which we were enabled to clear, and attempted to keep the ship from drifting on shore.

The whole of the 1st and 2nd of March, we anxiously hoped for a change. Our fatigues had been constant and excessive. Many had been severely bruised by being thrown down the hatchway by the violent jerks of the ship. I was particularly unfortunate in receiving three falls, which at length disabled me from going on deck. We had shipped several heavy seas that would have proved destructive to almost any other ship. The water forced its way into every part of the vessel and kept everything afloat between decks.

About three o'clock the morning of the 3rd, an enormous sea broke over the ship and for an instant destroyed every hope. Our gun-deck ports were burst in, both boats on the quarters stove, our spare spars washed from the chains, our headrails washed away, hammock-stanchions burst in, and the ship deluged and waterlogged. One of the prisoners exclaimed that the ship's broadside was stove in and that she was sinking. This alarm was greatly calculated to increase the fears of those below. Many were washed from the spar to the gun-deck, and from their hammocks, and did not know the extent of the injury. They were greatly alarmed, but the men at the wheel and some others, who were enabled by a strong grasp to keep their stations, distinguished themselves by their coolness and activity after the shock. I took this opportunity of advancing them one grade.

And now we began to hope for better times. For the sky became serene and the wind fair, and we were every moment receding farther from the influence of the dreary and inhospitable climate of Cape Horn. We passed the parallel of Chili on the 5th, and our sufferings appeared at an end.

It was my intention to look into Mocha, a small unin-
habited island on the coast of Chili about eight leagues
distant from the coast. It was settled in the early part of
the last century by the Spaniards and was deserted by
them, perhaps in consequence of the terrors excited by
the buccaneers. The island is now frequented by vessels
engaged in smuggling and in the whale fishery, as well
as those employed in catching seals, great numbers of
which are always to be found on the rocks and small
keys. It is a most desirable place for vessels to touch at
after doubling Cape Horn.

The land is high and may be seen at a great distance.
As soon as the ship anchored, the boats were got out, and
myself and several of the officers went on shore. The
sea was beating furiously against the beach and rocks
that skirt the shore, and it was some time before we could
find a landing place.

As we had seen, with our spyglasses, several hogs and horses on shore, I permitted the officers and the most careful of the men to take muskets with them. In the course of a few hours, we had killed and got down to the boats ten hogs with some very young pigs. Seeing a drove of horses coming along, and everyone being anxious to fire, I directed the men to conceal themselves behind the boats that were hauled on the beach and not to fire until I had fired, intending to reserve my shot until all could fire without the least danger of accident.

I fired and was succeeded by a volley. One horse was crippled, and the seamen ran forward with clubs to knock him down. They had hold of him when a young officer who was nearsighted ran forward and, seeing the group of sailors about the animal, supposed it to be horses and fired. Unhappily, the ball passed through the breast of James Spofford, the gunner's mate, one of the best and most trusty men in my ship. It is impossible for me to express what were my feelings when the poor fellow said, with the utmost composure and a firm voice, "Sir, you have shot me! I am a dying man; take me to the boat."

The distress of the officer on the occasion was beyond description. Doctor Hoffman was on shore and gave us little hope for his life, as the ball had entered the right breast and come out near the backbone. Had it not been for this dreadful accident, we should have been much delighted with our excursion on shore, as it not only afforded us a pleasant recreation after our excessive fatigues at sea, but enabled us to procure a fresh mess for all hands. The horsemeat, however, was generally preferred to the hogs', it being much fatter and more tender. The hogs proved tough and had an unpleasant flavor, though I heard no complaints among the sailors on that subject, as their stomachs were perhaps less delicate.

I have no doubt that in the few hours we were on shore, we were the cause of the death of at least a dozen horses, and double the number of hogs, that made their escape after being wounded. From the great number of bones that are scattered in every direction on the island, I have reason to believe that the same cruel warfare has been pursued by other navigators who have touched there. The animals are so numerous that one good marksman could more than supply a ship's company of 300 men with fresh provisions without making such unnecessary destruction among them. It is greatly to be lamented that visitors to this island should indulge themselves in such wanton cruelty as must, in time, deprive navigators of those refreshments.

I now considered myself in a good position to meet vessels plying between Conception and Valparaíso. As neither the health of the crew, the state of my provisions, nor the distresses of the ship rendered my going into port absolutely necessary, I determined to keep the sea a while longer in hopes of meeting some of the enemy's ships and thereby obtaining such supplies as would render it entirely unnecessary to make ourselves known on the coast until we were about quitting it.

We were surrounded by whales in great numbers, which gave us strong hopes of soon meeting some of the vessels engaged in catching them. The whales generally go in schools along the coast, and the whalers keep in pursuit of them, following their tracks north and south. We also saw many seals and birds, in greater numbers than at any time during our passage except while in the neighborhood of Mocha.

Nothing was to be seen but a wide expanse of ocean, bounded on the east by the dreary, barren, and iron-bound coast of Chili, at the back of which the eternally snow-capped mountains of the Andes reared their lofty heads. There was, altogether, presented to us a scene of gloomy solitude far exceeding anything I ever before experienced.

On the afternoon of March 13th, we made the point, three or four leagues to the southwest of the bay of Valparaíso, called by the Spaniards Quaranmilla [Curanmilla]. After doubling the point at the distance of half a league, we perceived some scattering rocks lying some distance from shore and shortly afterward opened into a handsome bay with a fine, sandy beach where we perceived some fishing boats. Wishing to have some communication with them, I hoisted the English ensign and pennant and a jack for a pilot, but none of them appeared disposed to come alongside. With the exception of the few cattle that grazed on the arid rocks, two huts, and the miserable-looking fishermen, the coast here had the same appearance as the rest we had seen. It was in vain that we sought for those handsome villages, well-cultivated hills, and fertile valleys which we had been prepared to meet in this part of the world.

The whole coast is skirted by a black and gloomy rock, against the perpendicular sides of which the sea beats with fury. At the back of this rock, the country appears dreary beyond description. Yellow and barren hills, cut by torrents into deep ravines and sprinkled sparingly here and there with shrubs, but not a tree was to be seen of any size on this whole extent of coast. When the weather was clear, we always saw the Andes. As these were never clear of snow, they were not calculated to give us a more favorable impression of the interior.

The next point which presented itself was the Point of Angels, which, I had learned, formed the western point of the bay of Valparaíso. As we rounded this point, I sought with my glass the city of Valparaíso or some proofs of our approach to it. First, a long, sandy beach on the opposite side offered itself to my view. Next, a large drove of mules coming down the side of the mountain by a zigzag pathway, and in an instant afterward, the whole town, shipping with their colors flying, and the forts burst out, as it were, from behind the rocks, and we found ourselves becalmed under the guns of a battery prepared to fire into us. The scene presented to us was as animated and cheerful as it was sudden and unexpected. Had I not hoisted English colors, I should have been tempted to run in and anchor.

A moment's reflection induced me to believe it would not be advisable to do so, as several large Spanish ships, with their sails bent and in readiness for sea, were lying in port. As those vessels were beyond doubt bound to the northward, and in all probability to Lima, I concluded on keeping the sea a few days longer to give them time to get out, in order that intelligence might not be given by them of an American frigate in this part of the world.

On the morning of the 15th, we furled all sails and put our drags into operation to get into the harbor. In the meantime, I dispatched Lieutenant Downes to inform the governor that we were an American frigate greatly in need of supplies of every kind, that our wants were augmented by the loss of our storeship off Cape Horn, and that we threw ourselves on his hospitality. I was induced to use this artifice from a knowledge of the unaccommodating disposition of the Spaniards and their jealousies respecting foreign vessels that enter the ports of their American possessions.

Before I had got to anchor, however, the captain of

the port, accompanied by Lieutenant Downes, came on board in the governor's barge with an offer of every civility, assistance, and accommodation that Valparaíso could afford. To my astonishment, I was informed that they had shaken off their allegiance to Spain and that the ports of Chili were open to all nations. Our arrival was considered the most joyful event, as their commerce had been much harassed by corsairs from Peru sent out by the viceroy of that province to capture all American vessels destined for Chili. Five of the corsairs had captured several American whalers and sent them for Lima only a few days before my arrival.

After anchoring, I saluted the town with 21 guns, which were punctually returned. Immediately after this I waited on the governor, who gave me the most friendly and unceremonious reception. On my passing the American armed brig *Colt*, she fired a salute of nine guns, which was returned by the *Essex* with seven. I had not been long with the governor before I discovered that I had, happily for my purpose, got among staunch republicans, filled with revolutionary principles and apparently desirous of establishing a form of government founded on liberty. The captain of the port, whose name I do not recollect, was a sterling, honest patriot and spoke his sentiments boldly. He evidently felt as those feel who are determined to be free, appeared sensible he had yet much to do, and, I am sure, was resolved to do the utmost to emancipate his country.

A courier was immediately despatched by the American deputy vice-consul to Santiago, capital of Chili, to inform Mr. Poinsett, the American consul general, of our arrival in the port of Valparaíso. Arrangements were made for getting our wood, water, and provisions on

board. I directed a daily supply of fresh beef and vegetables, fruit, and bread for the crew.

All the dry provisions were put up in hides. The
flour was better secured in them, and more closely
packed, than it could possibly be in barrels. The use the
Chileans make of hides is astonishing. Most of the furni-
ture for their mules and horses, and their houses, and, on
some parts of the coast, even their boats, or balsas, are
made of this article. When used for balsas, two hides,
each cut something in the form of a canoe, with the seam
upward, are blown up by means of a reed and stopped
together. A piece of board is then laid across to sit on,
and on this frail machine the Chileans venture a considerable distance to sea. The *laque,* for which they are
so famous, is formed of a very long strip of hide with a
running noose. Their dexterity in using it, in catching
animals at full speed, is surprising. Every pack-horseman
and driver of a jackass is furnished with one, and they
never fail to throw it over the neck of the animal wanted.

On the 17th Captain Munson, of the American brig in
port, arrived from St. Jago [Santiago], bringing me a
letter from the consul general. Captain Munson was
asked by the consul to inform me that, in a political
view, they considered our arrival as the most happy
event. The bells had been rung the whole day, and il-
luminations had taken place the evening after our arrival was announced—it was generally believed I had
brought from my country nothing less than proposals for
a friendly alliance with Chili and assurances of assistance
in their struggle for independence. This idea I felt no
disposition to do away with.

By the time I completed arrangements for provisioning
the *Essex*, I was informed that the governor intended
returning my visit. I consequently went on board to receive him and on his arrival with a numerous suite of officers, saluted him with 11 guns. It appears that many of
them had never seen a frigate, this being the first that
had entered the port. The visit lasted about two hours,
during which time they viewed every part of the ship.
Although she appeared under great disadvantage from
having been so long at sea and from the tempestuous
passage around Cape Horn, still, they were much pleased
and astonished that Anglo-Americans, as they styled us,
could build, equip, and manage ships of so large a size.

The governor, before he left the ship, invited myself
and officers to a party for the next evening and expressed
great regrets that we had not arrived sooner. They had
had, the evening before, great rejoicings in consequence

of a victory gained by their troops over those of Peru. It seems that a small, unimportant fortress belonging to the latter had fallen into the hands of the Chileans.

Agreeable to the governor's invitation, we attended his party, where we found a much larger and more brilliant assemblage of ladies than we expected. We found much fancy, and considerable taste, displayed in their dress and many of them, with the exception of teeth, very handsome both in person and in face. Their complexion was remarkably fine, and their manners were modest and attractive.

This was our first impression on entering a room containing perhaps 200 ladies, to whom we were perfect strangers. Minuets were introduced; country dances followed; and the ladies had the complaisance and patience to attempt with my officers what they had never before seen in the country, a cotillion. The intricacies of their country dance were too great for us to attempt; they were greatly delighted in by those who knew them, and admitted a display of much grace.

With their grace, their beauty of person and complexion, and with their modesty we were delighted and could almost fancy we had gotten among our own fair countrywomen. But in one moment the illusion vanished. The *ballas de tierra,* as they are called, commenced. They consisted of the most graceless and at the same time fatiguing movements of the body and limbs, accompanied by the most indelicate and lascivious motions, gradually increasing in energy and violence until the fair one, apparently overcome with passion and exhausted with fatigue, was compelled to retire to her seat.

They disfigure themselves most lavishly with paint, but their features are agreeable, and their large dark eyes are remarkably brilliant and expressive. Were it not for their bad teeth, occasioned by the too liberal use of the matti, they would be thought handsome, particularly by those who had been so long out of the way of seeing any women.

The matti is a decoction of the herb of Paraguay, sweetened with sugar and sucked through a long silver tube. To the use of this beverage the Chileans are perfect slaves. The taste is agreeable, but it occasions terrible havoc among the teeth. We returned on board our ship pleased with the novelties of a Chilean ball.

All were busily engaged until the 20th in getting on board our supplies. On the meridian of that day, we had completed our water and, with the exception of a few small articles, had as much provisions on board as the day we left the United States. As the next day was Sunday and we all required some relaxation from our fatigues, I determined to devote it to pleasure and invited the ladies and gentlemen of Valparaíso to spend the afternoon on board the ship.

The consul general had arrived from St. Jago accompanied by Don Lewis Carrera, the brother of the Chilean president, and others. They all dined on board my ship on Saturday and were saluted with 11 guns. On Sunday about three o'clock, myself and officers were on shore with our boats to take the ladies on board the ship, she having been previously prepared for their entertainment. We had all laid aside our national and religious prejudices and devoted ourselves entirely to the pleasures of the day when, at the moment we were on the point of embarking with them, an officer informed me that a large frigate had appeared in the offing and, on perceiving us, had hauled in for the harbor.

We all immediately left our fair Chileans and, without any ceremony, jumped in our boats and repaired on board. I soon perceived that the strange ship was a 32-gun frigate, gave orders to cut the cables, and in an instant the *Essex* was under a cloud of canvas. But as the breeze, which had until this moment blown, now failed, we got all our boats ahead and towed out of the harbor. In the course of an hour we were alongside the stranger, who proved to be a Portuguese sent around by the government at Rio de Janeiro for the purpose of getting a supply of flour for Lisbon.

As there was every expectation of an engagement, the consul general, several Americans and Spaniards, and Don Lewis Carrera came on board to share with us the dangers. The latter appeared to us a spirited youth and, as he had never been in any engagement of importance, was evidently anxious to partake of one. His constant request of me was to board the stranger, and his disappointment was great when he discovered the Portuguese flag. We could perceive the hills crowded with men, women, and children—all equally and perhaps more anxious than Don Lewis—to see the fight. Among them, as it afterward proved, were our fair guests, who frankly acknowledged that a sight of a sea engagement would have had more charms for them than all the entertainment we could have afforded them on board the ship.

The day being far advanced, I gave up all thought of returning to port that night and stood off to sea, endeavoring to get to windward. Don Lewis, as well as his servants who accompanied him, soon became excessively sick. However warlike he might have felt when he first came on board, he was now as helpless as an infant. We succeeded, by the help of our drags, in getting to our anchors early next morning and were more fortunate in finding the buoys we had put to our cables than I expected.

An invitation was brought for us to dine and spend the evening with the governor, who, we could perceive by the flags about the battery in front of his house, had made great preparations for the occasion. We were informed that the entertainment was given us by the order and at the expense of the superior government of Chili. The company was seated in an extensive tent, handsomely and fancifully decorated with the flags of different nations, and the ground covered with rich carpets. The dinner was served up in silver plate and consisted of at least 20 changes. By the time the third course had been removed, we had cause to regret that we had not reserved our appetites for some of the delicacies which we perceived were likely to succeed the substantial food of the first course, which we had begun upon with keen appetites. When the wine began to circulate, and the Chilean officers to feel the ardor of their patriotism, such flaming toasts were given as to make them think it prudent to retire.

As the ball was to succeed the dinner in the tent, we walked around with the governor to look at the fortifications. On our return we found the ladies assembled, dressed in all their splendor and unusually disfigured with paint. The night was spent with much hilarity, and at one o'clock in the morning, we repaired on board.

We now prepared to weigh our anchor, but the arrival of an American whaleship that had been carried into Lima and there liberated occasioned some little delay. I was desirous of obtaining the news from her. The captain, on coming on board, informed me that a few days before, he had spoken with two English armed whalers, one off the island of Mocha and the other off the harbor of Conception. Three other American whalers were in company, and the English ships were the first to give them the intelligence of the war. They informed them that they had no orders to capture American vessels but were in daily expectation of authority to that effect. The captain also informed me that several English whaleships were cruising among the Galápagos Islands and off the harbor of Payta [Paita] on the coast of Peru. He represented our whale fishers, which were very numerous, as in a helpless and unprotected state and entirely exposed to attack and capture by the armed English ships carrying from 14 to 20 guns and well manned. He stated that as sometimes our whaleships kept the sea for six months at a time, most of them were ignorant of the war and would fall an easy and unsuspecting prey to the British ships. After receiving this intelligence, I got under way and proceeded to sea with a fresh breeze from the southward, steering northwest to get an offing from the land.

During our stay in Valparaíso, two Spanish ships had sailed for Lima, and the certainty that they would give intelligence of us to the enemy made our speedy departure all the more necessary. From all accounts, the coast of Peru, and from there to the Galápagos, is the favorite fishing ground of the British whalers. I intended proceeding to the latter place before the British agent at Lima could give them intelligence of my arrival in this sea. It seemed beyond a doubt that they would conjecture that my designs were not confined to doubling Cape Horn merely for the pleasure of visiting Valparaíso.

The customs of the inhabitants of Valparaíso differ so materially from our own that I cannot help noticing a few particulars that struck me as the most singular. At all their dinner entertainments, the principal guest is placed at the head of the table, the host on one side of him and the hostess on the other. Their principal business seems to be to make the guest eat as much as possible.

The matti is taken with little regard to delicacy or cleanliness. When the cup containing it is brought in, one of the company blows into it through a silver tube until a high froth is produced. It is then considered properly prepared. The same matti and tube is passed around the room, and each one in turn takes a draught of it with apparent relish and delight. It is also a practice for one glass of water, one spoon, or one cigar to be served to the whole company. A Chilean lady would consider it a high indecorum to be seen walking arm in arm with a gentleman. Their refinement is so great that it is thought indelicate even to accept his hand in any way except in dancing, when, to be sure, everything like delicacy is laid aside. They are, however, extremely hospitable and attentive to strangers, even if they have their peculiar customs which seem strange to us.

On the 23rd of March, 1813, the Essex sailed toward the
northwest out of Valparaíso. For the next six months,
she cruised off the coast of Peru and among the islands
of the Galápagos chain. Two days out of port, she met
with the American whaleship Charles, Captain Gardner, out of Nantucket. Captain Gardner told Captain
Porter that his ship, along with the American whaleships
Walker and Barclay, had been attacked two days previously by a Spanish and an English ship off Coquimbo.

The Essex made all sail for that port and captured
the "Spanish" vessel, which proved to be the Peruvian
privateer Nereyda. She had, in truth, taken the whaleships, but she had been driven from her prizes by a
British letter-of-marque ship. The Nereyda, however, had
on board as prisoners Captain West of the Walker and
some of the crew of the Barclay, who told Porter that
the Americans had been plundered of everything by the

Peruvian ship. Also, that both ships, with full cargoes of whale oil, had been returning to America after long voyages and had known nothing of the war until the time of their capture.

The next morning Porter dismantled the Nereyda *by having all her guns, ammunition, small arms, and light sails thrown overboard, leaving only her topsails and courses to take her back to port. He liberated the Americans and directed the* Nereyda's *captain to proceed to Lima with a letter to the viceroy in which Porter protested the ship's attack on American commerce, calling it "piratical conduct."*

Porter then sailed northward on the coast of Peru and recaptured the Barclay, *Captain Randall. Randall elected to remain with the* Essex *for protection so that his ship would not fall again into the hands of the Peruvians. Captain Gardner sailed with the* Charles *for Coquimbo, 300 miles north of Valparaíso, there to place himself under the protection of the Chilean government.*

Both American whaling captains had advised Porter that the Galápagos Islands were the favorite cruising ground of British commercial ships. Also, that there were at least 20 British whalers in those seas, all fine ships of not less than 400 tons burden, whose cargoes in England would be worth $200,000 each.

To effect the capture and destruction of these British vessels, as well as the protection of American whaleships, the Essex *sailed for the islands, with Porter having made certain changes in the appearance of the frigate:*

We were employed in disguising our ship, which was done by painting her in such a manner as to conceal her real force, exhibiting in its stead the appearance of painted guns. Also, by giving her the appearance of having a poop and otherwise so altering her as to make her look like a Spanish merchant vessel.

On the morning of the 18th of April, I stood to the westward with a pleasant breeze from the east which ran us as far as the harbor of Charles Island [Santa María] in the Galápagos. On arriving opposite to it, we could perceive no vessels. Understanding that ships which stopped there for refreshments such as turtle and land tortoise, and for wood, were in the practice of depositing letters in a box near the landing place, I dispatched Lieutenant Downes to bring off any such letters as might be of use to us, should he find any.

He returned in about three hours with several papers taken from a box he found nailed to a post over which was a black painted sign, "Hathaway's Postoffice." From these papers I obtained information that six British whaleships had put in there last June. There were also letters giving information that the American ships *Perseveranda*, Captain Paddock, and the *Sukey*, Captain Macy, had touched there. Considering Captain Macy's letter as a rare specimen of orthography, I hope I shall be pardoned for giving an exact copy of it.

"Ship *Sukey*, John Macy, 7½ months out, 150 barrels, 75 days from Lima. No oil since leaving that port. Spanyards very savage. Lost on the Braziel bank John Sealin, apprentice to Captain Benjamin Worth. Fell from the foretop sail yard in a gale of wind. Left *Diana*, Captain Paddock, 14 day since, 250 barrels. I leave this port this day with 250 turpen, 8 boat load wood. Yesterday went up to Patts Landing east side. To the starboard hand of the landing 1½ miles saw 100 turpen 20 rods apart. Road very bad. Yours forevir, John Macy. June 14, 1812."

The harbor at Charles Island is formed on the northwest by a projecting point off which lies a remarkably high, black, ragged rock, which, from its appearance, I have been induced to call Rock Dismal. The landing here is very good. At the time Lieutenant Downes was on shore, a torrent of very fine water, many feet deep, discharged itself near the beach. As it was raining constantly while he was on shore and the mountains were completely capped with clouds, it was evident that the stream owed its existence to temporary rains alone. This opinion was also confirmed by some person who had bountifully left near the postoffice a cask of water for persons who might be there in distress.

The island is mountainous, as are all the Galápagos, and is covered with trees from 15 to 20 feet in height, scattered with considerable regularity on the sides of the hills. Every mountain and hill is the crater of an extinguished volcano, and thousands of smaller fissures, which have burst from their sides, give them the most dreary, desolate, and inhospitable appearance imaginable. The islands appear unsuited for the residence of man or any other animal that cannot, like the tortoises, live without food or draw its subsistence entirely from the sea.

It may be seen by Captain Macy's letter that on the east side of the island there is another landing, which he calls Pat's Landing. This place will probably immortalize an Irishman named Patrick Watkins who, some years since, left an English ship and took up his abode on this island. He built himself a miserable hut about a mile from the landing, in a valley containing about two acres of ground capable of cultivation—perhaps the only spot on the island which affords sufficient moisture for the purpose. Here he succeeded in raising potatoes and pumpkins in considerable quantities, which he generally exchanged for rum or sold for cash.

The appearance of this man, from the accounts I have received of him, was the most dreadful that can be imagined—ragged clothes scarce sufficient to cover his nakedness and covered with vermin, his red hair and beard matted, his skin much burned from constant exposure to the sun, and so wild and savage in his manner and appearance that he struck everyone with horror.

For several years this wretched being lived by himself on this desolate spot without any apparent desire than that of procuring rum in sufficient quantities to keep himself intoxicated. At such times, after an absence from his hut of several days, he would be found in a state of perfect insensibility, rolling among the rocks of the mountains. He appeared to be reduced to the lowest grade of which human nature is capable and seemed to have no desire beyond the tortoises and other animals of the island except that of getting drunk.

But this man, wretched and miserable as he may have appeared, was neither destitute of ambition nor incapable of undertaking an enterprise that would have appalled the heart of any other man. Nor was he devoid of the talent of rousing others to second his hardihood. He by some means became possessed of an old musket and a few charges of powder and ball, and the possession of this weapon probably first stimulated his ambition. The first human being that fell his way happened to be a Negro who was left in charge of a boat belonging to an American ship that had touched there for refreshments. Patrick came down to the beach where the boat lay, armed with his musket, now his constant companion. In an authoritative manner, he directed the Negro to follow him. On his refusal, he snapped his musket at him twice, which luckily missed fire. The Negro, however, became intimidated and followed him.

Patrick now shouldered his musket, marched off before, and, on his way up the mountain, exultingly informed the Negro he was henceforth to work for him and become his slave. On arriving at a narrow defile and perceiving Patrick off his guard, the Negro seized the moment, grasped him in his arms, threw him down, tied his hands behind, shouldered him, and carried him to the boat. When the crew arrived, Patrick was taken on board the ship.

An English smuggler was lying in the harbor at the same time, the captain of which sentenced Patrick to be severely whipped on board both vessels. He was afterward taken on shore, handcuffed, by the Englishmen, who compelled him to make known where he had concealed the few dollars he had been enabled to accumulate from the sale of his potatoes and pumpkins, which they took from him. But while they were busy destroying his hut and his garden, the wretched being made his escape. He concealed himself among the rocks in the interior of the island until the ship had sailed, when he ventured from his hiding place and, by means of an old file which he drove into a tree, freed himself from the handcuffs.

He now meditated a severe revenge but concealed his intentions. Vessels continued to touch there and Patrick, as usual, to furnish them with vegetables. But from time to time he was enabled, by administering potent draughts of his darling liquor to some of the men, and getting them so drunk that they were rendered insensible, to conceal them until the ship had sailed. Finding themselves entirely dependent on him, they willingly enlisted under his banner, became his slaves and he the most absolute of tyrants. By this means he augmented the number to five, including himself, and every means was used by him to procure arms for them, but without effect.

While Patrick was meditating his plans, two ships, an American and an English vessel, touched there and applied to Patrick for vegetables. He promised them the greatest abundance, provided they would send their boats to his landing and their people to bring them from his garden, informing them that his rascals had become so indolent of late that he could not get them to work. This arrangement was agreed to—two boats were sent from each vessel and hauled on the beach. The crews all went to Patrick's habitation, but neither he nor any of his people was to be found. After waiting until their patience was exhausted, they returned to the beach, where they found only the wrecks of three of their boats, which were broken to pieces, and the fourth one missing.

The crews succeeded, after much difficulty, in getting around to the bay opposite their ships, where some other boats were sent to their relief. The commanders of the ships, apprehensive of some other trick, saw no security except in a flight from the island, leaving Patrick and his gang in quiet possession of the boat. But before they sailed, they put a letter in a keg giving intelligence of the affair and moored it in the bay. There it was found by Captain Randall, but not until he had sent his boat to Pat's Landing for the purpose of procuring refreshments. As may be easily supposed, he felt no little inquietude until her return, when she brought him a letter from Patrick, to the following purport, found in his hut:

"Sir, I have made repeated application to captains of vessels to sell me a boat or to take me from this place, but in every instance met with a refusal. An opportunity presented itself to possess myself of one, and I took advantage of it. I have been long endeavoring, by hard labor and suffering, to accumulate wherewith to make myself comfortable, but at different times have been robbed and maltreated—and in a late instance by Captain Paddock, whose conduct in punishing me and robbing me of about $500 in cash and other articles neither agrees with the principles he confesses nor is such as his sleek coat would lead one to expect.

"On the 29th of May, 1809, I sail from the enchanted island in the *Black Prince,* bound to the Marquesas. Do not kill the old hen. She is now sitting and will soon have chickens. Father Oberlus."

Patrick arrived alone at Guayaquil in his open boat, the rest having perished for want of water or, as is generally supposed, were put to death by him on his finding the water to grow scarce.

From thence he proceeded to Payta, where he wound himself into the affection of a tawny damsel and prevailed on her to accompany him back to his enchanted island, the beauties of which he no doubt painted in glowing colors. But from his savage appearance, he was there considered by the police as a suspicious person, and, being found under the keel of a small vessel then ready to be launched, and suspected of some improper intentions, he was confined in Payta jail, where he now remains.

Probably owing to this circumstance, Charles Island, as well as the rest of the Galápagos, may remain unpopulated for many ages to come. And when we consider the issue which might be produced between a red-haired wild Irishman and a copper-colored mixed-blooded squaw, we need not any longer be surprised at the different varieties in human nature.

As the Essex *reconnoitered the various islands of the
Galápagos, searching for supplies of fresh water and
catching fish and turtles, the crew grew increasingly
despondent and dejected, despairing of capturing any
British whalers among the islands. At daylight on April
29th, Porter was roused from his cot, where he had
passed a sleepless and anxious night, by the cry, "Sail
ho! Sail ho!" echoing throughout the ship. The* Essex
*hoisted English colors and, later that morning, over-
hauled the* Montezuma, *her first British whaler, with
1,400 barrels of whale oil aboard. That same day, and in
short order, the* Essex *captured two additional British
whalers.*

The captured vessels proved to be, as I had expected,
the *Georgiana* of 280 tons and the *Policy* of 275 tons.
These three vessels, which we had taken with so little

trouble, were estimated to be worth, in England, upward of half a million dollars. The ease with which the last vessels were taken by our open boats gave us but a poor opinion of British valor, and the satisfaction which the possession of these valuable vessels gave us made us forget for a moment the hardships of Cape Horn.

It also afforded us a useful lesson, as it convinced us we ought not to despair of success under any circumstances, however unfortunate they might appear. Slight murmurings had on one or two occasions been heard from some of the crew, occasioned by our want of success heretofore. With a view to preventing this in the future, I considered it advisable to inculcate this maxim by the following note:

"SAILORS AND MARINES,

"Fortune has at length smiled on us, because we deserved her smiles, and the first time she enabled us to display FREE TRADE AND SAILORS' RIGHTS, assisted by your good conduct, she put in our possession near half a million of the enemy's property.

"Continue to be zealous, enterprising, and patient, and we will yet render the name of the *Essex* as terrible to the enemy as that of any other vessel before we return to the United States. My plans shall be made known to you at a suitable period.

"D. Porter, April 30, 1813."

The capture of these vessels relieved all our wants except one, to wit, the want of water. From them we obtained an abundant supply of cordage, canvas, paints, tar, and every other article necessary for the ship, of all of which she stood in great need, as our slender stock brought from America had now become worn out and useless. The vessels, when they sailed from England, were provided with provisions and stores for upward of three years and had not yet consumed half their stock. All was of the best quality.

We found on board the vessels, also, wherewith to furnish our crew with several delicious meals. They had been in at James Island [San Salvador] and had supplied themselves abundantly with those extraordinary animals, the tortoises of Galápagos, which properly deserve the name of the elephant tortoise. Many of them were of a size to weigh upward of 300 weight, and nothing, perhaps, can be more disagreeable or clumsy than they are in their external appearance. Their motion resembles strongly that of the elephant—their steps slow, regular, and heavy. They carry their bodies about a foot from the ground, and their legs and feet bear no slight resemblance to the animal to which I have likened them. Their necks are from 18 inches to 2 feet in length and very slender. The head is proportioned to it and strongly resembles that of a serpent.

But hideous and disgusting as is their appearance, no animal can possibly afford a more wholesome, lucious, and delicate food than they do. The finest green turtle is no more to be compared to them in point of excellence than the coarsest beef is to the finest veal. After once tasting the Galápagos tortoises, every other animal food fell greatly in our estimation. These animals are so fat as to require neither butter nor lard to cook them, and this fat does not possess that cloying quality common to that of most other animals. When tried out, it furnishes an oil superior in taste to that of the olive. The meat is the easiest of digestion, and a quantity of it can be eaten without experiencing the slightest inconvenience.

But what seems most extraordinary about this animal is the length of time it can exist without food. I have been well assured that they have been piled away among the casks in the hold of a ship, where they have been kept for 18 months. When killed at the expiration of that time, they were found to have suffered no diminution in fatness or excellence. They carry with them a constant supply of water in a bag at the root of the neck. The bag contains about two gallons and, on tasting, proved perfectly sweet and fresh. They are very restless when exposed to the heat and light of the sun, but will lie in the dark from one year's end to the other without moving. In the daytime they appear remarkably quick-sighted and timid, drawing their heads into their shells on the slightest motion of any object. They are entirely destitute of hearing, as the loudest noise, even the firing of a gun, does not seem to alarm them in the slightest degree. At night or in the dark, they appear perfectly blind.

After tasting the flesh of those animals, we regretted the numbers of them that had been thrown overboard by the crews of the vessels before their capture, to clear them for action. A few days afterward, we were so fortunate as to find ourselves surrounded by about 50 of them, which were picked up and brought on board. They had been lying in the same place where they had been thrown over, incapable of any exertion in that element except that of stretching out their long necks.

The *Georgiana* I found not only a noble ship, but well calculated for a cruiser. She sailed well and had been built for the service of the British East India Company and employed as a packet until this voyage. I therefore determined to equip and arm her completely and mounted on her the ten guns of the *Policy*, making her whole number now sixteen. To this were added two swivels and a number of heavy blunderbusses mounted on swivels, as well as all the muskets, pistols, cutlasses, and other military equipment we could find on board the other vessels. By this means I rendered her as formidable as any of the British letters of marque I could hear of in this ocean.

All this I did not undertake until I was well satisfied she could be well manned without reducing too much my own crew. A number of seamen already captured in the prizes had proffered their services to us. On inquiry, I found many of them to be Americans. They volunteered their services in equipping the *Georgiana* and freeing her from much of the lumber on board, consisting of empty casks and other cumbrous articles. The heavy brickwork and large iron boilers used for trying out the oil were taken down to give more room on her decks and relieve her from the great weight. This greatly improved her sailing.

The command of this vessel, now completely equipped for war, I gave to Lieutenant Downes, with a crew consisting of 36 of our own men and 5 of the men from the prizes, altogether 41 men. The remainder I kept on board the *Essex*, whose crew now amounted to 264 men, including officers and those on board the *Barclay*. The manning of this vessel enabled me to make some promotions on board my own ship from some of the most deserving of my crew, to fill up the vacancies occasioned by the petty officers sent on board her.

We now considered the sloop of war *Georgiana* no trifling augmentation of our own force. She was of the utmost importance to our safety, for, in the event of any accident happening to the *Essex* while cruising in a sea with which we were little acquainted, we could calculate on relief from the *Georgiana*. Added to this, she doubled the chance of annoying the enemy and might serve as an excellent decoy, as we were particularly careful not to change in the slightest degree her appearance as a whaler. On the 8th of May, she hoisted the American ensign and pennant and saluted the *Essex* with 17 guns, which was returned by our crew with three cheers.

Lieutenant Downes now made sail to the south, and I bore away for Charles Island, where I anchored in eight fathoms' water. The prizes and *Barclay* followed us in. As soon as the ship was moored, I went on shore to examine the letter box but found no new papers in it. I, however, saw unquestionable evidence of a vessel's having been in the harbor since we had left it, for the cask of water, barrel of bread, and other articles left there had been carried off, and no part of either remained but the hoops of the cask. Fresh tracks of men were plainly to be seen from the beach to the post office, where the articles were placed. And an impression was made in the sand as though a bag had been set down, near which were some whale-line yarns, part of which had been used, no doubt, for the purpose of tying it. All these circumstances left no doubt in our minds of their having been carried off by some whaleship. On comparing these yarns with those we had got from on board our prizes, they were known to be English. I now felt great regret that I had not kept the *Georgiana* with me until our arrival, that I could have dispatched her direct for Albemarle [Isabela] in search of the stranger.

I had heard of a spring in the interior of the island, which could be approached from a beach on the west side about six miles distant from the ship. To this place I proceeded next morning, taking with me two ten-gallon kegs to make the experiment with. We found the spring at the distance of three miles from the beach, and the water, after clearing it out, proved excellent. But it was found to be extremely laborious work getting it down to the beach, as our stoutest men were exhausted after taking down one keg each.

I thought it not unlikely that water might be found near the bay in which we lay. Well knowing the roving disposition of seamen, I determined to let a party go ashore to amuse themselves, confidently believing if water was to be found within two or three miles of us, it would be discovered by them. On their return at night I was not disappointed, for they informed me that they had found upward of 40 or 50 barrels of water lodged in the different hollows of the rocks about a mile and a half from the shore. The difficulties of getting to it were very great, but they did not doubt that each man would be enabled to bring down, in 10-gallon kegs, 40 gallons per day. I immediately caused casks to be landed and, by sending parties on shore daily, procured, while we lay here, 2,000 gallons—much of it, to be sure, of a filthy appearance, having a bad smell and taste, and filled abundantly with slime and insects. But to us it was a treasure too precious to lose, and the greatest industry was used to save every drop of it for fear that the sun, which was evaporating it rapidly, would cheat us of our prize.

Early in the morning of the third day of our arrival, a sail was discovered to the westward, standing in for the island. I immediately caused preparation to be made for sending the boats after her, as the wind was very light, but on her nearer approach, when she made her private signal, discovered it to be the *Georgiana*. Her arrival, though unexpected, gave me much pleasure. On Lieutenant Downes' coming on board, he informed me that, on doubling the southwest part of the island which we had supposed to be James, he had discovered several other small islands and had experienced rapid currents which had put the safety of his ship in jeopardy. He had been swept very near to a high rock which lies in a passage of about two miles wide, formed by the southwest part of the island and another, smaller island. It was with no little difficulty that he extricated himself from the dangers of rocks and breakers in this unknown navigation.

After Lieutenant Downes had been with me a short time, I dispatched him to Albemarle in pursuit of the stranger who had touched at the island before us. I directed him to stop at Charles Island as soon afterward as possible and, should he not find me there, to search at the foot of the stake to which the letter box is attached, where I should bury a bottle containing instructions for him.

After the *Georgiana* had left us, I proposed to Mr. Adams, the chaplain, that he should take two boats and proceed to the large island for the purpose of making an accurate survey of it. Mr. Adams, whose zeal for promoting geographical and mathematical knowledge does him great honor, grasped at the proposal with avidity, and at 4 P.M., supplied with a week's provisions and every necessary for the same period, he sailed on his voyage of discovery in a whaleboat belonging to the *Essex* and another belonging to the *Montezuma*. I directed them to be back to the ship between the fifth and sixth day from their departure.

That every person might be employed to the most advantage, I directed that those having charge of prizes should paint them and put them in good order in the expectation that they would bring a higher price among the Spaniards, to whom I intended offering them for sale at the first opportunity. They were noble ships, and a little paint added greatly to the beauty of their appearance.

While we lay here, I permitted all the prisoners to go on shore whenever they wished it, as many of them were affected with the scurvy. One in particular was so bad with it as to be scarcely able to move. But on getting him on shore, where he could procure a kind of sorrel and the prickly pear, and burying his legs in the earth every day, he was so far recovered before our departure that he could walk as briskly as any among us, assisting frequently in bringing down water and tortoises from the rocks and mountains.

On the 20th of May, in the morning, discovered the two whaleboats returning with Mr. Adams from the island they had been sent to survey. As I was apprehensive that they had exhausted their stock of water, I dispatched a boat with a supply, which proved very acceptable, as they had been 18 hours without any. Mr. Adams informed me that he had made a complete survey of the island and had determined the latitude and longitude of the principal points. From this island, James, Albemarle, Charles, and many others were to be seen. As this island was now destitute of a name and he could perceive no traces of its having been visited before, he highly complimented me by giving it the name of Porter's Island.

On the night of his return from Porter's Island, Mr. Adams fell in with a ship which he passed at the distance of gunshot. She bore much the appearance of an English vessel, had a tier of guns, and was bound toward Albemarle. I determined to run down for Banks's Bay to look for her. I not only hoped, by so doing, to secure a valuable prize, but expected to be enabled to get a supply of water from her, which was what we still stood more in need of than any other article whatever.

On the 27th of May we were abreast of Cape Essex, or
the south head of Albemarle. I intended now to go over
the cruising ground of the whalers with great care, as
Captain Randall had informed me that he had discovered
some of the garbage of whales floating on the surface of
the water near Hood's Island [Española], a certain indication of whalers' having been there lately. In order
that none should escape me, I caused the prizes to spread
off in different directions, keeping at signal distance. They
were to keep a good lookout, with orders to make a
signal to me in the event of their discovering any strange
vessel. I, however, directed them to close in with the
Essex at night, to guard against separation.

On the afternoon of the 28th, as we were standing in
to the northward with the *Montezuma* in tow, the *Barclay* looking out on our starboard, and the *Policy* on our
larboard quarter, the man on the lookout on board the

Essex discovered a sail right ahead. Immediately, the *Montezuma* was cast off and all sail made in chase. At sunset we could see her plainly from deck. As she was standing from us with all the sail she could crowd, I entertained no hopes of coming up with her in the night, for I had no doubt of her altering her course and thus eluding us. The wind continued fresh, and, believing she would change her course as soon as it grew dark, I hove to at 9 P.M. for the other vessels to come up. I directed the *Montezuma* to run northwest seven miles and then heave to, the *Barclay* to run the same distance to the east, and I intended sending the *Policy* to the southwest, but she did not come up in time. This arrangement, I hoped, would enable one or the other of the vessels to get sight of the chase in the morning.

The next day the *Montezuma* made a signal for a sail to the northward, and we hove away in pursuit of her with all the sail we could carry. It was not until two hours after we had given chase to her that we could discover her from our mastheads. About meridian the wind began to die away. The *Montezuma* was still between us and the ship and distant from us about six miles. I determined now that she should not again escape us, for I was fully convinced this was the same vessel we had chased the day before.

I directed three of the fastest rowing boats to be manned with as many armed men as they could carry and to proceed, under the command of Lieutenant Wilmer, to the *Montezuma* with orders to take three of that ship's boats and, before night, to proceed to take a station astern of the stranger. He was to keep sight of him, placing the other boats in a line astern of him so that a communication could be had by signal from the headmost boat to the *Montezuma,* and from thence to the *Essex.*

By this arrangement, I hoped to be guided by flashes in my pursuit of the enemy and prevent the probability of his escaping. I directed Lieutenant Wilmer not to make any attack on her unless it should prove perfectly calm, and then to row up with muffled oars and board her by surprise. To prevent any other mode of attack being made, I allowed them no other arms than a pistol, cutlass, and boarding ax each.

After the boats had left us, a breeze sprung up, which enabled us to continue the chase. As we soon passed the boats, I made a signal for the *Montezuma* to heave to and pick them up. As we approached the chase, the stranger hauled close on a wind to the eastward and shortly afterward hove about to stand for us. From her warlike appearance and the signals made by her, I supposed her to be an English sloop of war. She wore both the English ensign and pennant. I now made such preparations for action as my weak crew would admit of, directing the marines and topmen to lay by their muskets and all on board to take their stations at the guns. All my officers were away from the ship, but still I could not perceive that the small remains of my men had in time of need lost any of their wonted energy and zeal.

When alongside, I hoisted English colors and directed her commander to come on board, which order was soon complied with. At this instant another strange sail was descried from the masthead. A few men were taken out of our prize, which proved to be the British letter-of-marque ship *Atlantic*, Obediah Wier master, employed in whaling, and mounting six guns. As soon as the *Montezuma* came up, I threw some men on board the *Atlantic* with Lieutenant McKnight and sent her in pursuit of the other stranger to the northwest, while I steered more northerly. As the *Atlantic* was reputed to be the fastest sailer in those seas, I had no doubt, by these means, of rendering her capture certain.

Night was now fast approaching. We were doubtful whether we were near enough to keep sight of our new chase, which our prisoners informed us was another British letter of marque. As it grew dark, we once lost sight of her. We soon discovered her again by means of our night glasses, and, on her heaving about to elude us on the supposition that we could no longer see her, we soon got alongside of her. On our firing a shot at her, she hove to. I directed her commander to repair on board, which he refused to do until he knew who we were. I fired one shot between his masts to intimidate him, threatening him with a broadside if he did not repair on board immediately. This had the desired effect. He came on board prepared to meet in us an enemy.

The vessel proved to be the British letter-of-marque ship *Greenwich*, of ten tons, a prime sailer employed in the whale fishery. Her captain had taken in a good stock of Dutch courage, and, from the preparations that were made on board his vessel, there could be no doubt of his intentions to have fired into us had he not been intimidated by the shot we gave him between the masts. He expressed great regret that the *Atlantic* and his ship had not joined one another before their capture, as he believed they would have been more than a match for us. Indeed, considering the then weakened state of the crew, and the absence of every officer, it seems not unlikely, as they were in every respect well prepared for action, that they would have given us some trouble and rendered the capture of one of them at least doubtful.

I must here observe that the captain of the *Atlantic* (an American from Nantucket, where he has a wife and family), on his first coming on board the *Essex*, expressed his extreme pleasure on finding, as he supposed we were, an English frigate in those seas. He informed me that he had sailed from England under convoy of the frigate *Java* and had put into Port Praya a few days after the *Essex,* an American frigate, had left there—that the *Java* had sailed immediately in pursuit of her, and that it was the general belief the *Essex* had gone around the Cape of Good Hope.

I asked him how he reconciled it to himself to sail from England under the British flag and in an armed ship after hostilities had taken place between the two countries. He said he found no difficulty in reconciling it to himself, for, although he was born in America, he was an Englishman at heart. This man appeared the polished gentleman in his manners but evidently possessed a corrupt heart and, like all other renegades, was desirous of doing his native country all the injury in his power, with the hope of thereby ingratiating himself with his new friends. I permitted him to remain in his error some time but at length introduced him to the captains of the *Montezuma* and *Georgiana,* who soon undeceived him with respect to our being an English frigate. I felt great pity for these last two gentlemen and had made the evils of war bear as light on them as possible by purchasing of them, for the use of the crew, their private effects, consisting of slop clothing, tobacco, and spirits, for which they were sincerely grateful. But toward this man I could not feel the same favorable disposition, nor could I conceal my indignation at his conduct.

After the capture of the *Greenwich,* I informed her commander, John Shuttleworth, as well as Obediah Wier of the *Atlantic,* that I felt every disposition to act generously toward them. Shuttleworth was, however, so intoxicated and his language so insulting that it was with difficulty that I could refrain from turning him out of my cabin. Wier was more reserved during my presence there, but, duty requiring me on deck, he, in the presence of some of the officers, used the most bitter invectives against the government of the United States. He, as well as Shuttleworth, consoled himself with the pleasing hope that British frigates would soon be sent to chastise us for our temerity in venturing so far from home.

They were at length shown to the apartment allotted them, where, feeling, in some measure, restraint removed, they gave full vent to their anger and indulged in the most abusive language against our government, the ship, and her officers. They lavished on me, in particular, the most scurrilous epithets, giving me appellations that would have suited a buccaneer. They appeared to have forgotten they were prisoners and in my power, and that it would be more to their advantage to trust entirely to my generosity than to irritate me by such unprovoked abuse. However, I determined next day to make them sensible of the impropriety of their conduct and did so without violating either the principles of humanity or the rules of war. I let them feel that they were dependent entirely on my generosity, and this haughty Englishman, who thought to have terrified me with the name of Britain, and this renegade, who would have sacrificed the interests of his country, were now so humbled by a sense of their own conduct that they would have licked the dust from my feet had it been required of them to do so.

Our fleet now consisted of six sail of vessels, without including the *Georgiana*. On board the last captured vessels, I put a sufficient number of men to fight their guns, giving Lieutenant McKnight charge of the *Atlantic*,

The frigate *Essex*. This painting, dating from about 1801, is the only known contemporary painting of the *Essex*. It is believed the artist, Joseph Howard, was involved in building the ship in Salem in 1799.

Captain David Porter at the time of the cruise of the *Essex* to the Pacific during the War of 1812. This portrait now hangs in Bancroft Hall at the Naval Academy in Annapolis.

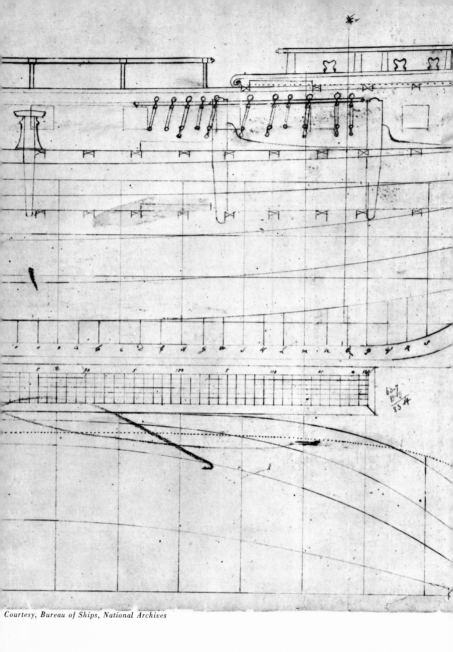

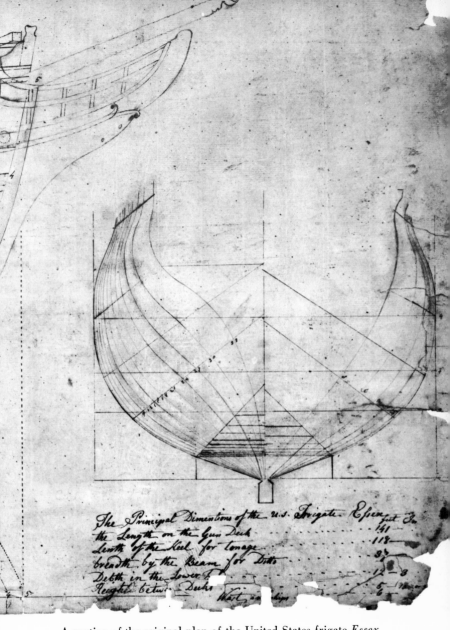

A portion of the original plan of the United States frigate *Essex*. She was built by Enos Briggs of Salem on a design prepared by William Hackett.

This engraving by William Strickland of the *Essex* and her prizes moored in Massachusetts Bay at Nuku Hiva, in the Marquesas, was taken from an original drawing by Captain Porter. It was one of the illustrations for Porter's *Journal of a Cruise*.

Quarter Deck.

David Porter Esqr. Comm^r.

John G Cowell Sailing Master

M. W. Bostwick, to attend Signals

James G Farragutt

T David Fittermary) Midship^n

T Henry W Ogden) & Aids

David H Porter

Joseph L Biggs - Mid^n & Aid.

(left)

This page, from the original quarter deck and watch bills of the *Essex* during her wartime cruise, shows Farragut's name as James. This was his name as a boy, and he later changed it to David, perhaps in honor of his foster parent.

(right)

Lieutenant John Downes very much as he must have looked during the War of 1812. From an oil painting by Jarvis.

The burning of the prize *Hector*, by naval artist William Bainbridge Hoff. Hoff illustrated David Dixon Porter's life of his father published in 1875.

A watercolor of the final battle of the *Essex* off Valparaíso, originally owned by Admiral Farragut and his son Loyall.

The *Victory*, from an engraving by William Strickland taken from a drawing by Captain David Porter, first illustrated Porter's *Journal of a Cruise*.

A fine engraving of Captain David Porter in later life, taken from the original painting by Chappell. The signature below is from a letter written by Porter to the Secretary of the Navy during the cruise.

and, for want of sea officers, I put Lieutenant Gamble of the marines in charge of the *Greenwich*. I had much confidence in the discretion of this gentleman. To make up for his want of nautical knowledge, I put two expert seamen with him as mates, one of whom was a good navigator.

Volunteers continued to offer from the captured vessels, and my force in those seas now consisted of: the *Essex,* mounting 46 guns and 245 men; *Georgiana,* 16 guns and 42 men; *Atlantic,* 6 guns and 12 men; *Greenich,* 10 guns and 14 men; *Montezuma,* 2 guns and 10 men; *Policy,* 10 men. Making a total of 80 guns and 333 men, together with 1 midshipman and 6 men on board the *Barclay.* My prisoners amounted in number to 80. I divided them among the different ships, allowing them full allowance of provisions on condition of their giving assistance in working, and found them as useful as our own men in navigating the prizes. Thus, our whole number, including the prisoners, amounted to 420 and all in good health with the exception of some of the latter who were slightly affected with the scurvy.

The *Greenwich* proved to be the vessel that had been seen by Mr. Adams and the *Atlantic* the one that had taken from Charles Island the barrel of water and bread. This, the captain informed me, was done with a view of preventing his men from deserting, a circumstance which he greatly apprehended while they could be certain of finding a supply of those articles on the island.

It seems somewhat extraordinary that British seamen should carry with them this propensity to desert even into merchant vessels sailing under the flag of their nation and under circumstances so terrifying. Yet I am informed that their desertion while at Charles Island has been very common, even when there was no prospect whatever of obtaining water but from the bowels of the tortoises. This can only be attributed to that tyranny so prevalent on board their ships of war, which has crept into their merchant vessels and is there aped by their commanders. Now, mark this difference. While the *Essex* lay at Charles Island, one fourth of her crew was every day on shore and all the prisoners who chose to go. I even lent the latter boats, whenever they wished it, to go for their amusement to the other side of the island. No one attempted to desert or to make his escape. Whenever a gun was fired, every man repaired to the beach, and no one was ever missing when the signal was made.

Soon after, a most disagreeable circumstance took place, which, for the credit of the ship and of the officers of the American Navy generally, I wish it was not necessary to relate. As, however, it took place in the presence of our prisoners, who, no doubt, will make their representations of it with suitable embellishments, I conceive it proper to give a correct statement of the affair.

Lieutenant W., the second lieutenant, had in two or three instances been intoxicated, so much so as to compel me once to arrest him, as at such times his conduct had been extremely violent and offensive to all on board. But as this officer possessed many good qualitites and was much esteemed for his goodness of heart, his brother officers interceded for him, pledging themselves for his future good conduct. On a solemn promise from him that he would abstain from ardent liquors while he continued under my command, I relieved him from his arrest with an assurance that for another similar offense his authority should forever cease on board the *Essex*.

During one of my short absences, Lieutenant W. felt himself relieved from all restraint and could not resist the opportunity of again indulging in his horrid propensity, which an abstinence of many months had rendered only more ungovernable and to which he was strongly invited by Captain Shuttleworth, the prisoner who had conducted himself so improperly.

On my return Lieutenant W. was officer of the deck, and, fearing that I would discover his situation, he left the deck as soon as I entered the ship. He retired to his stateroom while I was engaged in conversation with the first lieutenant. Not knowing his condition, I sent repeatedly for Lieutenant W., who was reported to me as lying in his cot and could not be made to answer. He had once before attempted suicide, and I felt apprehensive that he had now made an attempt on his life.

I went to his stateroom, where I found him in his cot with his face down. After considerable difficulty and repeated efforts to move him, I succeeded in turning him over. He requested me to let him alone. I told him I was determined to investigate the cause of his conduct. He then sprang up and with great violence of gesture and language demanded to know what I intended to do, observing at the same time that he had been drunk and that he had not had time to get sober. I informed him that he was under arrest. He asked me how long. I told him as long as the cruise lasted. He then seized a pistol, which he attempted to load, observing that neither myself nor any other should have the satisfaction of arresting him. Not knowing whether he intended to use the pistol against me or himself, I grasped him and took it from him. He then attempted to load another, which was also taken from him.

He assured me that he had no intentions of using the pistol against me—that, if I would permit him, he would blow his own brains out, observing that he would put an end to his existence before morning.

I sent for a guard and had his room searched for arms, which were all taken away from him. I afterward confined him there, with two sentinels at the door with orders not to permit him to leave it. When the arms were taken out, he refused to go into the room until some violence was used to compel him. However, he became at length pacified and, by morning, dejected and penitent. He declared that he had violated his promise to me as well as to his brother officers who had interceded for him and that he could not survive the shame. He had formed the determination of putting an end to his existence the first opportunity that presented itself.

The ship now being left with only one sea lieutenant, it became necessary to supply the deficiency, and the more so since I had suffered much lately from the want of officers. I therefore ordered Lieutenant McKnight to join the *Essex*, placing Mr. Adams, the chaplain, in charge of the *Atlantic*. I appointed Midshipman J. S. Cowan acting fourth lieutenant, giving the appointment of sailing master to Midshipman Odenheimer. To supply their places on board the prizes I put the younger midshipmen, boys from 12 to 15 years of age, making them nominally prizemasters, with careful seamen, in whom I could confide, to take care of them.

"IT WAS EVIDENT THAT HE WAS A PIRATE."

Lieutenant Downes had left with the Georgiana *on May 12th to reconnoiter throughout the Galápagos chain of islands. On his return on June 24th, he was accompanied by two prizes, the* Hector *and the* Catherine. *A third captured ship, the* Rose, *had been given up to her captain on condition that he would proceed to St. Helena with all the prisoners. All of her guns and most of her cargo of oil were thrown overboard.*

Porter's fleet now numbered nine ships. As the Atlantic *was far superior to the* Georgiana *in size, appearance, sailing, and every other qualification necessary for a cruiser, Porter ordered 20 guns to be mounted on her, removed Lieutenant Downes and his crew to that ship, and placed Mr. Adams in charge of the* Georgiana.

The Atlantic *was renamed the* Essex Junior *and the crew increased to 60 men. The* Greenwich, *with all cumbrous articles removed, was converted into a storeship.*

On the 4th of July a salute of 17 guns was fired from the Essex, Essex Junior, *and* Greenwich *in commemoration of the independence of the United States. The day, Porter adds, was spent in the utmost conviviality—a sufficient quantity of spirits was procured from the prizes and issued to the crew.*

On the 9th of July Lieutenant Downes with the Essex Junior *escorted to Valparaíso the prizeships* Hector, *Catherine,* Policy, *and* Montezuma *and the recaptured American whaleship* Barclay. *He had directions to leave the* Barclay *there and to sell the others to the best advantage or make such disposition of them as he judged most advantageous.*

It was at this time and under these circumstances that young Midshipman Farragut was given his first real command, and he tells the story in this way:

"I was sent as prizemaster to the *Barclay*. This was an important event in my life, and when it was decided that I was to take the ship to Valparaíso, I felt no little pride at finding myself in command at 12 years of age.

"This vessel had been recaptured from a Spanish *guarda costa*. The captain and his mate were on board, and I was to control the men sent from our frigate, while the captain was to navigate the vessel. Captain Porter, having failed to dispose of the prizes as it was understood he intended, gave orders for the *Essex Junior* and all the prizes to start for Valparaíso. This arrangement caused great dissatisfaction on the part of the captain of the *Barclay*, a violent-tempered old fellow. When the day arrived for our separation from the squadron, he was furious and very plainly intimated to me that I 'would find myself off New Zealand in the morning,' to which I most decidedly demurred. We were lying still while the other ships were fast disappearing from view—Captain Porter going north and the *Essex Junior,* with her convoy, steering to the south for Valparaíso.

"I considered that my day of trial had arrived, for I was a little afraid of the old fellow, as everyone else was. But the time had come for me to at least play the man; so I mustered up courage and informed the captain that I desired the main topsail filled away in order that we might close with the *Essex Junior.* He replied that he would shoot any man who dared to touch a rope without his orders, that he would go his own course and had no idea of trusting himself with a d——d nutshell. Then he went below for his pistols.

"I called my right-hand man of the crew and told him my situation. I also informed him that I wanted the main topsail filled. He answered with a clear 'Aye, aye, sir,' in a manner which was not to be misunderstood, and my confidence was perfectly restored. From that moment, I became master of the vessel and immediately gave all necessary orders for making sail, notifying the captain not to come on deck with his pistols unless he wished to go overboard. I would have had very little trouble in having such an order obeyed.

"I made my report to Captain Downes on rejoining the *Essex Junior.* Captain Randall also told his story, in which he endeavored to persuade Downes that he only tried to frighten me. I replied by requesting Captain Downes to ask him how he succeeded, and to show him that I did not fear him, I offered to go back and proceed with him to Valparaíso. He was informed that I was in command, he being simply my adviser in navigating the vessel in case of separation. So, this being settled and understood, I returned to the *Barclay* and everything went on amicably up to our arrival in Valparaíso."

When Lieutenant Downes arrived in Valparaíso, he found that a declaration of war had taken place between Chili and Peru and that an entire stop had been put to the commerce between the two governments. For this reason, it was impossible for him to sell the prizes. He dispatched the Policy *for America with a full cargo of whale oil and moored the* Montezuma, Hector, *and* Catherine *in the harbor at Valparaíso. He then sailed with the* Essex Junior *to rejoin Captain Porter.*

In the meantime, Captain Porter sailed for Charles Island in the Galápagos, keeping with him the storeship, Greenwich, *and the* Georgiana. *The following day, he captured three additional British whalers, the* Charlton, Seringapatam, *and* New Zealander.

The captain of the *Seringapatam,* William Stavers, gave me more pleasure than any other commander who fell into my hands, for, besides having the finest British ship in those seas, he had the character of a man of great enterprise. He had already captured the American whaleship *Edward* of Nantucket and might have done great injury to American commerce in those seas.

Although Stavers had come to the Pacific on a whaling voyage, he had given but little attention to that object while there was a hope of meeting American whalers. On my requiring of this man that he should deliver to me his commission, he, with the utmost terror in his countenance, informed me that he had none with him. He added that he was confident his owners had taken one out for him and had no doubt sent it to Lima, where he expected to receive it. It was evident that he was a pirate, and I did not feel that it would be proper to treat him as I had done other prisoners of war. I there-fore ordered him and all his crew in irons. But after inquiring of the American prisoners I found on board the prize as to the manner in which they had been treated by the crew of the *Seringapatam,* and being satisfied that they as well as the mates were not to blame for the conduct of their commander, I liberated them from confinement, keeping Stavers only in irons.

I determined to give the *Charlton* up to the captain, as she was an old vessel and a dull sailer, on the con-dition that he should land all my prisoners at Rio de Janeiro. To this contract he, as well as the captain of the *New Zealander,* bound himself by oath. After taking from her a cable and such other articles as were necessary for us, and sending all her guns and military equipment on board the *Seringapatam,* I dispatched the *Charlton* on the 19th with 49 prisoners.

The mates and sailors, however, expressed their deter-mination not to go to Rio de Janeiro with the ship for fear of being pressed on board a British ship of war. They were very solicitous that I would allow them whale-boats and let them take their chance in them, declaring that any fate, however dreadful, would be preferable to a servitude in His Majesty's Navy. To this I would not consent, lest it might be supposed I had turned them adrift in the middle of the Pacific. They then requested to remain with the *Essex.* I did not wish to be encum-bered with them and would not agree to this proposal. They at length grew turbulent, and I was apprehensive I should have to use some coercive measures in order to restore to the captains the necessary authority to keep them in order. But, after my reasoning with them on the impropriety of their conduct, they became more orderly and made sail to the southward, giving us at their departure three hearty cheers and many best wishes for our success and safe return to America.

As the *Seringapatam* proved to be a fast-sailing ship and was in every respect calculated for a man of war (and, indeed, was built for one, in India, for Tippoo Sahib), I determined to render her as formidable as possible, that, in case of any accident happening to the *Essex,* our cruise might not be entirely broken up. With this view, I sent the carpenters and gunners to work on her, and in a few days she was completely equipped, with 22 guns mounted. I gave her in charge to Mr. Terry, master's mate, with directions not to separate from us. I placed the *New Zealander* under the charge of Mr. Shaw, the purser, with similar instructions.

On the 24th I determined to send the *Georgiana* to the United States, for several reasons:

In the first place, I considered that on her arrival on our coast, the season would favor her getting in. I calculated it would require five months for her to reach it, which would bring it to the dead of winter and consequently at a time when ships of war cannot cruise on the northern ports on account of tempestuous weather.

Secondly: The ship had a full cargo of spermaceti oil, which would be worth, in the United States, about $100,000 and could not be sold on this coast without making great sacrifices.

Thirdly: I was desirous of getting rid of Stavers. He was a man of great cunning and considerable observation, and, however desirous I might be of concealing my intentions, I was apprehensive that some circumstances might lead him to conjecture rightly as to my future views. In order to put it entirely out of his power to obtain and give such information as was calculated to benefit the enemy or frustrate my plans, I thought it advisable (as I had always intended sending him to America for trial) to dispatch him in the *Georgiana*.

Fourthly: Repeated applications had been made to me by the officers to overlook the offense of Lieutenant W. His activity and bravery on board the *Greenwich*, during her action with the *Seringapatam*, gave me a secret inclination to do so without violating my word or incurring the imputation of inconsistency. To reinstate him on board the *Essex* was entirely out of the question, but I saw no obstacle to giving him command of the *Georgiana* to take to America. This was an arrangement which gave general satisfaction to everyone, as I at the same time liberated him from arrest and withdrew the charges I intended to present against him.

Fifthly: The period was fast approaching when the times of many of my crew were to expire. I was desirous of sounding them as to their views on the occasion, and with this object I permitted the crew of the *Georgiana* to be made up of those whose period of enlistment would expire next month. I had the great satisfaction to observe but little desire on the part of any to return before the *Essex*. A crew, however, was made up for her, but composed, by no means, of the best of my men.

Every arrangement being made, the *Georgiana* left us on the 25th of July, giving us a salute and three cheers at her departure. We had an opportunity, by this vessel, of writing to our friends and enjoyed, in pleasing anticipation, the effect that the news of our great success would produce in the United States.

At seven o'clock on the morning of the 28th of July, I
discovered a strange sail to the eastward. On viewing
her with my spyglass from the topgallant yard, she appeared to be close on a wind under our topsails with
fresh breezes, while our ships were lying nearly becalmed. A light air, however, springing up from the westward, we made all sail in chase, but the rapidity of the
current was so great that we soon lost all sight of the
stranger. At meridian, we were driven so close to the
shore that we entertained the most lively apprehensions
for the safety of the ship, and it was with some considerable difficulty that we escaped getting on shore. As
the sea was beating with great violence against its perpendicular and inaccessible sides, this apprehension was
calculated to produce reflections of no very agreeable
nature.

As soon as the ship was out of danger, we began to

think again of our chase. We were not in the habit of readily giving up a pursuit while it was probable the chase was an enemy, our uncommon success having taught us to believe that to see and to capture were one and the same thing. I firmly believed that the stranger was a British whaleship, and every advantage was taken of the light airs which prevailed all day and that night to endeavor again to get sight of her.

The next morning at half past seven, she was discovered to the northeast from the masthead, standing on a wind toward us and across our bows. At half past nine she was directly to windward of us, distant about seven miles. As she had discovered that we were a frigate and, no doubt, had intelligence of our being in this quarter, she hoisted American colors and made all sail from us. The winds coming in light, inclinable to calm, we made use of our drags and found considerable advantage from them. But, from the constant labor requisite to work them, our people became very much harassed and, finally, worn out with fatigue.

By the greatest exertions, we had approached within four miles of the chase when he got his boat ahead to tow his ship, with a view, as I supposed, of running her on shore, which was not far distant. To prevent his effecting this, I dispatched the gig and the whaleboat with a few good marksmen to drive them from their boats, but with the most positive orders to make no attempt on the ship. They soon succeeded in driving the boats alongside the ship but found great difficulty in keeping out of range of his shot, as he had mounted two guns on his forecastle, with which he kept up a constant fire on our boats. He hauled down his American colors and hoisted English.

At four o'clock on the afternoon of the 30th, both ships

were perfectly becalmed at the distance of three and a half miles from each other—our two boats lying ahead of the enemy and preventing his boats from towing; my crew so worn out with fatigue as to be incapable of working the drags to any advantage; the enemy with English and we with American colors flying. I considered him as already our own and that the ceremony of taking possession was all that was now requisite.

I could plainly perceive that his force did not exceed 10 guns and 30 men, and, as any alternative was preferable to working the drags any longer, I, to the great joy of everyone on board, gave orders for attempting her with the boats. They were soon hoisted out, manned, armed, and dispatched after her. The enemy, seeing so formidable a force coming against him, fired a few guns, apparently with a view of intimidating. Finding that they continued to advance, he ceased firing and hauled down his colors.

The boats had now got within three quarters of a mile of him when a fresh breeze sprang up from the eastward, with which he made all sail to the northward, hoisted his colors, and fired at our gig and whaleboat as he passed, which in return gave him volleys of musketry. Before sunset he was hull down ahead of us, while we were lying the whole time perfectly becalmed.

Our boats continued the chase, with the hope that it would again fall calm, and made flashes occasionally to guide me in the pursuit, which I was enabled to pursue when the breeze struck me at sundown. I came up with the boats at nine o'clock at night. We had lost all sight of the enemy, and the apprehension of losing all my boats and officers, and the greater part of my crew, induced me to heave to and take them on board. At daylight, seeing nothing of the enemy, I hove about to rejoin my prizes.

Nothing, perhaps, could equal our disappointment in not taking this vessel. We had already calculated with such confidence on her as to arrange her prize crew and were exulting that we had completely destroyed, with the exception of one vessel more, the British whale fishery on the coast of Peru. Great as our mortification was that he should make his escape after so long a chase, we consoled ourselves in some measure with the reflection that this was the first enemy who had ever escaped us and that his escape was due to a fortuitous circumstance.

On the morning of August 4th at six o'clock, we were between James Island and Albemarle, beating the passage, which is about 18 miles wide, to reach the harbor. We came to anchor in the bay at half past two in six fathoms' water, within a quarter of a mile of the middle of the beach, over a soft sandy bottom. I caused the prizes to moor ahead and astern of the *Essex,* in a line along the shore, so close as to prevent an enemy from passing inside of us in case of attack. I caused the pinnace and cutters to be hoisted out, rigged, and anchored in shore, to be in constant readiness in the event of an enemy appearing.

After every arrangement was made that could suggest itself to me for the safety of the ships, as well for offensive as defensive operations, I commenced making those little repairs which every ship requires in a greater or lesser degree on going into port after being some time at sea. I caused the *Seringapatam* to be painted exactly like the *Essex* and gave to the *Greenwich* the aspect of a sloop of war, hoping at some future period to derive some advantage over the enemy by the deceptions I should be enabled to practice by means of these changes.

It became necessary to take all our powder on shore for the purpose of sunning and sifting it. I discovered, to my great regret, that nearly one third of that contained in casks was damaged and unfit for use, in consequence of the water having entered the magazine, either during our passage around Cape Horn or, which is more likely, while our rudder was in a damaged state off the coast of Patagonia. We were, however, enabled to get a considerable quantity from the *Seringapatam,* which, although it left that ship nearly destitute, in a great measure supplied our deficiency.

We here, after painting our ships, repairing our sails and boats, setting up our rigging, and doing various other jobs which could not conveniently be done at sea, began to lay in our stock of tortoises, the grand object for which every vessel anchors at the Galápagos Islands. Four boats were dispatched every morning for this purpose and returned at night, bringing with them from 20 to 30 each, averaging about 60 pounds. In four days we had as many on board as would weigh about 14 tons, which was as much as we could conveniently stow. They were piled up on the quarter-deck for a few days with an awning spread over to shield them from the sun, which renders them very restless, in order that they might have time to discharge the contents of their stomachs. They were then stowed below, as you would stow other provisions, and used as occasion required. No stock is so convenient for ships to take to sea as tortoises of these islands. They require no provisions or water for a year, nor is any further attention to them necessary than that their shells should remain unbroken.

I have now the painful task of mentioning an occurrence which gave me the utmost pain, as it was attended by the premature death of a promising young officer by a practice which disgraces human nature. The service at this time received an irreparable injury in this man's death. I shall, however, throw a veil over the whole previous proceedings and merely state that, without my knowledge, the parties met on shore at daylight and at the third fire Mr. Cowan fell dead. His remains were buried the same day in the spot where he fell, and the following inscription was placed over his tomb:

"Sacred to the memory of Lieutenant John S. Cowan, of the U.S. frigate *Essex*, who died here anno 1813, aged 21 years. His loss is ever to be regretted by his country and mourned by his friends and brother officers."

Prior to my leaving the place, I buried a letter for Lieutenant Downes in a bottle at the head of Mr. Cowan's grave and a duplicate of the same at a finger post, erected by me, for the purpose of pointing out to such as may hereafter visit the island the grave of Mr. Cowan. With the design of misleading the enemy, I left in a bottle, suspended at the finger post, the following note:

"The United States frigate *Essex* arrived here on the 21st July, 1813, her crew much afflicted with the scurvy and ship fever, which attacked them suddenly. She lost her first lieutenant, surgeon, sailing master, 2 midshipmen, gunner, carpenter, and 36 seamen and marines.

"She captured in this sea the following British ships: *Montezuma, Policy, Hector, Atlantic, Catherine, Rose, Charlton, Georgiana, Greenwich, Seringapatam,* and *New Zealander.* For want of officers and men to man them, the last 4 were burned. The *Rose* and *Charlton* were given up to the prisoners.

"The *Essex* leaves this in a leaky state, her foremast rotten in the partners and her mainmast sprung. Her crew have, however, received great benefit from the tortoises and other refreshments the island affords.

"Should any American vessel, or, indeed, a vessel of any nation, put in here and meet with this note, they would be doing an act of great humanity to transmit a copy of it to America in order that our friends may know of our distressed and hopeless situation and be prepared for worse tidings if they should ever again hear from us."

While we lay at the bay in James Island, which I called Cowan's Bay, we put our goats on shore to graze, keeping a person to attend them through the day and give them water. As they were all very tame and kept about the landing place, we every night left them on shore. There was one young male and three females, one of which was of the Welsh breed and was with young by a Peruvian ram with five horns which we had taken in one of our prizes. The rest were of the Spanish breed. The sheep were also left on shore with them.

The morning after they had been there several days and nights, the person who attended them went on shore as usual to give them their water, but no goats were to be found. They had all, as with one accord, disappeared. Several persons were sent in different directions for two or three days to search for them, but without success. They undoubtedly took to the mountains in the interior, where unerring instinct led them to the springs from whence the tortoises obtain their supply. Unmolested as they will be in the interior of this island, to which they will no doubt confine themselves on account of the water, it is probable their increase will be very rapid. Perhaps nature, whose ways are mysterious, has embraced this first opportunity of stocking the island with a race of animals who are, from their nature, almost as well enabled to withstand the want of water as the tortoises. Perhaps she has so ordained it that the breed which shall be produced between the Welsh goat and the Peruvian ram shall be better adapted to the climate than any other.

There was one fact which was noticed by myself and many others the day preceding the departure of the goats and must lead us to believe that something more than chance directed their movements. It was observed that they all drank an unusual quantity of water. The old Welsh goat, particularly, did not seem satisfied until she had drunk upward of half a gallon, which, for a goat, it must be admitted, is an extraordinary draught. The others drank a quantity not far short of it, which seems as though they had determined to provide themselves with a supply that would enable them to reach the mountains.

On the 22nd I directed the prizes to proceed into a small cove inside of Narborough [Fernandina], which I shall call Port Rendezvous, with orders to await my arrival in six weeks. After scrubbing our ship, we, on the 3rd of September, stood over for Hood's Island, where we anchored in a bay on the north side. This bay I called Rodgers' Bay and the island forming it Rodgers' Island, in honor of Commodore Rodgers.

We lay here until the 8th in hopes of the arrival of Lieutenant Downes from Valparaíso or the appearance of some stranger, as this is the island which all whaleships endeavor to make. Previous to quitting the bay, I sent on shore a letter for Lieutenant Downes. It was buried in a bottle at the back of the sand beach at the foot of a post on which was nailed a board with the following inscription: "S.X., Anno Dom., 1813." And now, having accomplished the main object for which I had come to this island, I determined to cruise a few days to the windward of it.

At daylight on the 15th, the men at the masthead descried a strange sail to the southward. On going aloft with my glass, I could perceive that she was a ship and under very easy sail, apparently lying to. As she was directly to windward of us, I did not wish to alarm her by making much sail, as I believed her to be an English whaler. I consequently directed the fore and main royal yards to be sent down and the masts to be housed, the ports to be shut in, and the ship to be disguised in every respect as a merchantman. I kept plying to windward for the stranger under easy sail as he continued to lie to, drifting down on us very fast. At meridian we were sufficiently near to ascertain that she was a whaleship and then employed in cutting up whales. From her general appearance, some were of the opinion that it was the same ship that had given us so long a chase and put us to so much trouble. She was, however, painted very differently, and from her showing no appearance of alarm, I had my doubts on the subject.

I had got possession of some of the whalemen's signals and made one which had been agreed on between a Captain William Porter and the captain of the *New Zealander,* should they meet. I did not know but this might be Captain Porter's ship and that the signal might be the means of shortening the chase by inducing him to come down for us.

At one o'clock we were at the distance of four miles

when she cast off from the whales she had alongside and made all sail from us. Everything was now set to the best advantage on board the *Essex,* and at four o'clock we were within gunshot when, after our firing six or eight shot at her, she bore down under our lee and struck her colors.

She proved to be the British letter-of-marque ship *Sir Andrew Hammond,* pierced for 20 guns, commissioned for 16, but had only 12 mounted, with a complement of 36 men. She was commanded by the identical Captain Porter whose signal I had hoisted. But the most agreeable circumstance of the whole was that this was the ship we had formerly chased. The captain assured me that our ship had been so strangely altered that he supposed her to be a whaleship until we were within three or four miles of him, and it was too late to escape. Nor did he suppose her to be a frigate until we were within gunshot and, indeed, he never would have suspected her to be the same ship that chased him before, as she did not now appear above one half the size she did formerly.

The decks of this ship were full of the blubber of whales they had cut in but had not had time to try out. The captain informed me there was as much as would make from 80 to 90 barrels and that it would require three days to try out. But, as I understood it would be worth between $2,000 and $3,000, I determined that it should not be lost. I therefore put on board her a crew who had been accustomed to the whaling business and placed the ship in charge of Mr. Adams, the chaplain, with directions to try out and stow away the oil with all possible expedition. But, that he might do it more conveniently, I directed him to bear up for Port Rendezvous, the harbor where the prizes lay.

I beat up for Port Rendezvous against a fresh land

breeze and anchored there in 15 fathoms' water, a little outside of the prizes. I here moored head and stern and lay perfectly secure from all winds. The officers and crews of the prizes, as may naturally be supposed, were greatly rejoiced to see me. They were heartily tired of being confined to this most desolate and dreary place, where the only sounds to be heard were the screechings of the sea fowls and the melancholy howling of the seals. Their rest was much disturbed the first few nights of their arrival there, but after that the seals abandoned their haunts. Then even their absence was regretted, as their noise, disagreeable as it was, served to break in upon that irksome monotony, which, for the want of occupation and amusement, became to them insupportable.

The time was now arriving for me to expect Lieutenant Downes. I therefore determined to fill up my water and provisions from my prizes and wait until the 2nd day of October, which was the period fixed for my departure. I had determined, should he not arrive in that time, to leave letters for him and proceed to the Marquesas, where I intended to clean my ship's bottom, overhaul her rigging, and smoke her to kill the rats. They had increased so fast as to become a most dreadful annoyance to us by destroying our provisions, eating through our water casks, thereby occasioning a great waste of our water, getting into the magazine and destroying our cartridges, eating their way through every part of the ship, and occasioning considerable destruction of our provisions, clothing, flags, sails, etc.

It had become dangerous to have the rats any longer on board. As it would be necessary to remove everything from the ship before smoking her, and probably to heave her out to repair her copper, which, in many places, was coming off, I believed that a convenient harbor could be found among the islands that would answer our purpose as well as furnish the crew with vegetables and fresh provisions. By this means, we should be enabled to save our salt provisions.

The *Sir Andrew Hammond* having an abundant supply, I hauled her alongside and took from her as much beef, pork, bread, water, wood, and other stores as we required. But what was more acceptable to our men than all the rest, I took from her two puncheons of choice Jamaica spirits, which was greatly relished by them, as they had been without any ever since our leaving the coast of Peru. Whether it was the strength of the rum or the length of the time they had been without, I cannot say, but our seamen were so affected by the first allowance served out to them that many were taken to their hammocks perfectly drunk. Indeed, there was scarcely a seaman in the ship but that was in some degree intoxicated. To prevent a recurrence of a similar scene, I caused it to be considerably diluted before it was again served out. This, however, did not prevent some from getting intoxicated, as the rum was such a rarity to them and so far superior to what they had been accustomed to drink that an allowance of it would command almost any price. As several found the ways and means to make their purchases, drunkenness could not be effectively stopped. I did not conceive it expedient to resort to rigid measures. Considering the long time they had been deprived of it without murmuring and the great propensity of seamen for spirituous liquors, and as no evil was likely to result from a little inebriety, provided they conducted themselves in other respects with propriety, I was disposed to give them a little latitude.

We had, ever since our arrival at Port Rendezvous, kept men constantly on the lookout from the top of the hill forming the north side of the port, which commanded a view of both bays. Here we had a flagstaff erected and suitable signals established, to which the attention of everyone was now turned. On the meridian of the 30th, a signal was made for a ship in the south bay, and shortly after, another was hoisted for a boat standing in for the harbor. A fresh breeze springing up, she soon rounded the southeast point, and, from her general appearance, all believed it to be the *Essex Junior,* which opinion was soon confirmed by the appearance of Lieutenant Downes. Her arrival was welcomed by our seamen with three cheers, and, at 3 P.M., the *Essex Junior* anchored near us.

By this ship, I received several letters from our consul general at Valparaíso, our consul at Buenos Aires, and newspapers. Though the papers were of old dates, they contained news of the greatest interest to us.

We obtained intelligence by them of the re-election of Mr. Madison to the presidency and various changes in the executive departments of the government. Also, the most satisfactory account of the successes of our Navy in every instance where our ships had encountered an enemy of equal force. My letters from our consul at Buenos Aires informed me that on the 5th of July the British frigate *Phoebe,* of 36 guns, and the *Raccoon* and *Cherub,* sloops of war of 24 guns each, accompanied by a storeship of 20 guns, had sailed from Rio de Janeiro for the Pacific Ocean in pursuit of the *Essex.* I also obtained intelligence that several British merchant ships were soon expected at Valparaíso from England with valuable cargoes. Mr. Downes informed me that he had left one there richly laden and on the point of sailing for India. As I believed it highly probable that the ship bound to India would touch at the Marquesas on her way thence, I thought it likely that, by a speedy arrival there, I should be enabled to capture her. None of the information I had received could induce me to alter my original plan of going to the Marquesas. The repairs and smoking of my ship were paramount to every other consideration, and I knew of no place where I could be more likely to do it undisturbed.

And now, having nothing to detain us but a head wind, we made every preparation for getting under way, which we did on the afternoon of the 2nd of October, when a light breeze sprang up which we took advantage of to get out of the harbor. On the 6th, finding that some of my prizes were dull sailers and occasioned considerable delay, I determined to dispatch the *Essex Junior* ahead of me for the Marquesas. I directed Lieutenant Downes to proceed to St. Christiana and afterward to join me at Port Anna Maria in the island of Nooaheevah [Nuku Hiva], which place I also appointed as a rendezvous for all the other vessels in case of separation.

As we had little to employ our people about during our run, and as I believed at this time, more than any other, I had much to apprehend from the scurvy getting among them, I considered it necessary to rouse them from that listlessness and apathy into which the human mind is apt to fall when destitute of employment. All were ignorant of the place of our destination or my intentions—I saw no prospect of evil resulting from making them known. I have ever considered that cheerfulness is a more powerful antiseptic than any other known, and I determined to apply one of the doses which, I believe, had heretofore greatly contributed to preserve the health of my men. The following note was communicated to them. Those who know the disposition of sailors may readily conceive the effect it produced. For the remainder of our passage, they could talk and think of nothing but the amusements and novelties which awaited them in this new world.

"We are bound to the Western Islands, with two objects in view:

"First, that we may put the ship in a suitable condition to enable us to take advantage of the most favorable season for our return home.

"Secondly, I am desirous that you should have some relaxation and amusement after being so long at sea, as, from your late good conduct, you deserve it.

"We are going among a people much addicted to thieving, treacherous in their proceedings, whose conduct is governed only by fear and regulated by views to their interest. We must put nothing in their power, be ever on our guard, and prevent, by every means that can be used, disputes and difficulties with them. We must treat them with kindness but never trust them, and be most vigilant where there is the greatest appearance of friendship. Let the fate of the many who have been cut off by the savages of the South Sea islands be a useful warning to us.

"It will require much discretion and good management to keep up a friendly intercourse with them. In the regulations that I shall lay down for this object, I shall expect the hearty concurrence of every person under my command.

"Disputes are most likely to arise from traffic with them. To prevent them, I shall appoint a vessel for the express purpose of trading and shall select an officer and four men to conduct all exchanges. Every other person is positively forbidden to traffic with the natives, except through the persons so selected to conduct the trade.

"No canoes or male natives will be permitted to come alongside the *Essex* or any other vessel except the trading ship, on any account, unless it may be the chiefs whom I may designate. And if every person exerts himself to carry on the work of the ship, as well as to enforce the above regulations and such others as I may from time to time adopt, I shall allow you time to amuse yourselves on shore. But this indulgence shall cease the moment I shall discover any relaxation in vigilance or industry.

"D. Porter, October, 1813."

At daylight of October 25th, I discovered the island of
Nooaheevah, which I shall hereafter call Madison's Island, and which bore up from us west, not more than
ten leagues distant. At the dawn of day, I made the
signal to bear up for the anchorage and stood in for the
east point side of the weather bay. This point is steep,
and the coast from thence to the north appears iron-
bound and inaccessible.

Shortly after anchoring, we discovered a boat coming
from the shore with three white men in her, one of whom
was perfectly naked with the exception of a cloth about
his loins. As his body was all over tattooed, I could not
doubt his having been a long time on this or some other
island. I supposed them to be seamen who had deserted
from some vessel here, and, under this impression, would
neither permit them to come alongside the ship nor allow
any person to have conversation with them. I was pro-

voked to find such characters as I suspected them to be, in a place where I had least expected to find any but the natives. I directed them to leave the ship.

Several canoes had come out toward us, but on the whites joining them, they all paddled to the shore. On their reaching the beach, considerable numbers of the natives assembled around them, armed with clubs and spears, and I felt somewhat apprehensive that I had committed an error in not treating the strangers with more urbanity. I was desirous of establishing with the natives the most friendly intercourse, and, to correct my error as soon as possible, if I had made any, I directed four boats to be manned and armed and, with a party of marines, proceeded for the shore. The beach was abandoned at our approach, but, on landing, I was met by one of the persons who had come off in the boat. To my great astonishment, I discovered him to be a midshipman of the United States Navy named John M. Maury, who had left the United States on furlough for Canton in the ship *Pennsylvania Packet*. He sailed with Lieutenant Lewis for this island to procure sandalwood and remained here for several months. After completing the cargo, the ship sailed for Canton, leaving Mr. Maury with a party to collect a cargo for the return. The ship was expected in about two months, but the news of the war, of which we brought the first accounts here, destroyed all expectations of seeing it again. Mr. Maury and his party saw no other prospect of getting away, and he requested me to take them on board. To this I consented, provided Lieutenant Lewis should not return before my departure.

The man before spoken of, who came off to the ship naked, was called Wilson, an Englishman by birth. He had been for many years among the group of Marquesas. He spoke their language with the same facility as his own and had become in every respect, except in color, an Indian. The looks of Wilson had strongly prejudiced me against him, but I soon discovered him to be an inoffensive, honest, good-hearted fellow, well disposed to render every service in his power. His only failing was a strong attachment to rum.

Wilson soon became a great favorite with me, as well as with every other person. He proved indispensably necessary to us, and without his aid I should have succeeded badly on the island. His knowledge of the people and the ease with which he spoke their language removed all difficulties in our intercourse with them. In all future interviews between me and the natives, Wilson is the organ of communication by which we are enabled to understand each other. I shall therefore in future deem it unnecessary to say I was assisted by an interpreter. It must always be understood I had one.

Observing the mountains surrounding the valley at Madison's Island to be covered with numerous groups of natives, I inquired the cause. I was informed that a warlike tribe called the Happahs, residing beyond the mountains, had been for several weeks at war with the natives of the valley of Tieuhoy [Taiohae], the Tayees. They had made several incursions into the valley, destroyed many homes and plantations, and killed a great number of breadfruit trees by girdling. I was also informed that they intended paying another visit that day, but it was supposed they were deterred by the appearance of the ships. I inquired if it were possible to get a message to them and was informed that there were certain persons who were permitted to pass freely from one tribe to another. One such was pointed out to me, and I sent him to the Happahs to tell them that I had come with a force sufficiently strong to drive them from the island, to warn them to cease all hostilities so long as I remained among them, and to say that if they had hogs or fruit to dispose of, they might come and trade freely with us, as I should not permit the natives of the valley to injure or molest them.

To the natives of the valley, who listened attentively, I then addressed myself and assured them that I had come with the most friendly disposition—that I should protect them against the Happahs, should they again venture to descend from the mountains. I directed them to leave their spears, slings, and clubs at home in order that we might know them from the Happahs. I also told them I should consider all as my enemies who should appear armed in my presence.

All listened with much attention; their spears and clubs were thrown on one side. While I was using measures to get together my officers and men, who had wandered away in different directions, my attention was drawn to an object which at the moment presented itself. A handsome young woman of about 18 years of age, her complexion fairer than common, her carriage majestic, and her dress better and somewhat different from the other females', approached. Her glossy black hair and her skin were highly anointed with coconut oil, and her whole person and appearance neat and comely. On inquiry who this dignified personage might be, I was informed that her name was Piteenee, a granddaughter to the chief or greatest man of the valley, whose name was Gattanewa. She received my advances with a coldness and hauteur which would have suited a princess, and repelled everything like familiarity with a sternness that astonished me. Yet this lady, like the rest of the women of the island, soon followed the dictates of her own interest and formed a connection with one of the officers which lasted, with but little fidelity on her part, as long as we remained, showing herself on the whole a most notorious jilt.

Gattanewa, I was informed at the time of my landing, was at a fortified village on the top of one of the highest mountains. They have two of these strong places, one at the top of the mountain and the other in the valley, guarding one of the principal passes. The manner of fortifying those places is to plant closely on end the bodies of large trees, 40 feet in length, securing them together by pieces of timber strongly lashed across. At the back of this a scaffolding is raised, on which is placed a platform for the warriors, who ascend by means of ladders and thence shower down on their assailants spears and stones. I no sooner understood they had a chief than I was anxious to see him, and a messenger was accordingly dispatched. After collecting my people, I returned on board, where I found every person anxious for the ship to be got into port and secured. Probably the crew had heard from those who had been on shore of the friendly reception they had met with.

When the ship was moored, the shore was lined with natives of both sexes, but the females were most numerous, waving their white cloaks for us to come on shore. The boats were got out and proceeded to the shore, where, on landing, they were taken complete possession of by the women, who insisted on going to the ship. In a short time the *Essex* was filled with them, of all ages and descriptions, from 60 years to 10. Some were as remarkable for their beauty as others for their ugliness. They all appeared to be of the most common kind, and many of them, who had been in the habit of visiting ships which had formerly been in this place, had been taught by the seamen some few English words, which they pronounced too plain to be misunderstood.

The object of the greatest value at this as well as all the other islands of this group is whales' teeth. This I had understood while I was on shore, and, knowing that there were several of them on board the frigate, I determined to secure the whole of them at any price. I had been informed that hogs, the only animal food on the island, could be purchased for no other article. I succeeded in procuring nearly all on board by paying for them at the rate of $1 each. This strange ornament is worn suspended to the neck and sometimes cut to form ornaments to the ears. No jewel, however valuable, is half so esteemed in Europe or America as is a whale's tooth here. Some idea may be formed of the value in which they are held by the natives when it is known that a ship of 300 tons' burden may be loaded with sandalwood at this island at the price of ten whales' teeth of a large size. For these, the natives will cut it, bring it from the distant mountains, and take it on board the ship. This cargo in China would be worth near a million dollars.

Soon after, I was informed that Gattanewa had arrived. To show my respect for the chieftain, I sent him on shore a fine large English sow. This, I was informed, was the most acceptable present I could make him, excepting only a whale's tooth.

Gattanewa came on board in a boat, accompanied by Mr. Maury. I had seen several warriors since my arrival, many of them highly ornamented with plumes formed of the feathers of cocks and man-of-war birds and the long tail feathers of the tropic bird. Large tufts of hair were tied around their waists, their ankles, and their loins. They wore a cloak, sometimes of red cloth, but more frequently of white paper cloth formed of the bark of a tree, thrown not inelegantly over their shoulders. They wore in their ears large round or oval ornaments formed of whales' teeth, ivory, or a kind of soft and light wood whitened with chalk. From their neck suspended a whale's tooth or highly polished shell; and round their loins were several turns of the stronger kind of paper cloth, the end of which hangs before in the manner of an apron. This, with a black and highly polished spear of about 12 feet in length or a club richly carved and borne on the shoulders, constitutes the dress and equipment of a native warrior, whose body is highly and elegantly ornamented by tattooing. This is a faithful picture of a warrior, and of the chief of such warriors I had formed an exalted opinion.

But what was my astonishment when Gattanewa presented himself—an infirm old man of 70 years of age, destitute of every covering or ornament except a clout about his loins and a piece of palm leaf tied about his head. A long stick seemed to assist him in walking, and his face and body were as black as a Negro's from the quantity of tattooing which entirely covered them. His skin was rough and appeared to be peeling off in scales from the quantity of kava, an intoxicating root, in which he had indulged himself. As he had drunk freely of the kava before he made his visit, he appeared to be perfectly stupid. Such was the figure that Gattanewa presented.

After he had been a short time on deck, I endeavored to impress him with a high opinion of our force. For this purpose I assembled all my crew. It scarcely seemed to excite his attention. I then caused a gun to be fired, which seemed to produce no other effect on him than that of pain. He complained that it hurt his ears. I then invited him below, where nothing whatever excited his attention until I showed him some whales' teeth. This roused the old man from his lethargy, and he would not be satisfied until I had permitted him to handle, to measure, and count them over and over. After he had done this repeatedly, I put them away.

Shortly afterward I asked him if he had seen anything in the ship that pleased him—if he did, to name it and it should be his. He told me he had seen nothing which pleased him so much as one of the small whales' teeth, which I took out and gave him. This he carefully wrapped up in one of the turns of his clout, begging me not to inform any person that he had about him an article of so much value. I assured him I should not, and the old man threw himself on the settee and went to sleep. In a few minutes he awoke, somewhat recovered from his stupidity, and requested to be put on shore.

Previous to his departure, he requested me to exchange names with him and assist him in his war with the Happahs. To the first I immediately consented but told him I had come to be at peace with all on the island and that I wished to see him at peace with the Happahs. I told him that I should not engage in any hostilities unless the Happahs came into the valley, in which case I should protect him and his people. He told me they had cursed the bones of his mother, who had died but a short time since, and that, as we had exchanged names, she was now my mother and I was bound to espouse her cause. I told him I would reflect on the subject and did not think it necessary to make any further reply to the old man's sophistry.

I now unbent my sails and sent them on shore and landed my water casks, with which I formed a complete enclosure sufficiently spacious to answer all our purposes. The ship was hauled close in with the beach, and we began in good earnest to make our repairs. A tent was pitched within the enclosure and the place put under the protection of a guard of marines.

In the afternoon several officers went on shore to visit the villages. I perceived a large body of the Happahs descending from the mountains into the valley among the breadfruit trees, which they soon began to destroy. I immediately fired guns and made a signal for every person to repair on board. The firing of the guns soon occasioned them to halt, and shortly afterward the whole returned up the mountains. As the Happahs had descended to within half a mile of our camp and had succeeded in destroying 200 breadfruit trees, it became necessary to be more on our guard against their enterprise. I determined to be prepared for them. With this view, I caused one fourth of each ship's company to be landed every evening with their arms as a guard for the camp, allowing them at the same time to stroll about the valley and amuse themselves. I also caused a tent to be erected on shore for myself, believing that my presence there was necessary to preserve order. Also, my health required that I remain some time on shore after being so long confined to the ship.

I determined to let the Happahs see the effects of our cannon, to frighten them from committing further hostilities. Gattanewa had made daily applications for assistance, and I at length told him that if his people would carry a heavy six-pounder up to the top of a high mountain which I pointed out to him, I would send up men to work it and drive away the Happahs, who still kept possession of the hills. I landed the gun but did not suppose them capable of carrying it halfway to the place fixed on. I supposed, however, that it would terrify the Happahs, and, if it was attended with no other advantage, it would occupy the natives for a fortnight or two and keep them away from our camp. The numbers who resorted there had already given us some embarrassment and, I apprehended, would cause more.

On the gun being landed, I ordered a few shot to be fired, to convince them of the distance the shot would have effect. First, a shot was fired with the gun considerably elevated. They seemed much surprised at the length of time the shot remained in the air, and a general shout of admiration marked the time of its fall in the water. I then directed the gun to be fired so that the ball might skip along the surface of the water. At every bound of the shot, they gave a general shout of applause as if all were operated on the same impulse. Last of all, I directed her to be fired with grapeshot, which seemed to afford them more pleasure than all the rest. They hugged and kissed the gun, lay down beside it, fondled it with the utmost delight, and at length slung it to two long poles and carried it toward the mountain. On their first attempt to lift it with a few men, the weight seemed to astonish them. They declared it had stuck to the ground. They soon, however, raised it by additional numbers and bore it off with apparent ease.

Our men were now occupied in overhauling and refitting the rigging, and the duty of everyone allotted to him. No work was exacted from any person after four o'clock in the afternoon; the rest of the day was given to repose and amusement. An oven was also built on shore with bricks found on board the prizes, and, so long as we remained here, fresh bread of an excellent quality was issued every day to every person under my command. This was the cause of great saving of our hard bread, which it was necessary to reserve as sea stock. We now only wanted to fall on some substitute for salt provisions, as we had not yet been enabled to procure hogs in sufficient quantities to issue to the ships' companies, nor to catch fish with our seine, although we had made repeated trials. The natives did not appear willing to traffic for fruit or hogs.

The day after the gun was moved for the mountains, the chief warrior, named Mouina, was introduced to me. He was a tall, well-shaped man of about 35 years of age—remarkably active, of an intelligent and open countenance, and his whole appearance highly prepossessing. He had just left the other warriors in the fortified village and had come down to request a musket, which he called a *bouhi*, to be fired, that he might witness its effects. I fired several times at a mark, to show that I never failed of hitting an object the size of a man. I then directed the marines to fire by volleys at a cask, which was soon like a riddle.

Mouina appeared much pleased at the effect of our musketry and frequently exclaimed, *"Mattee! mattee!* (Killed! Killed!)"* The Happahs who were present, however, replied that nothing could persuade their tribe that *bouhies* could do them the injury that we pretended and that they were determined to try the effects of a battle. If they should be beaten, they would be willing to make peace, but not before. I informed them that they would not find me so ready to make peace after beating them as at present.

Gattanewa came to inform me that the gun was at the foot of the mountain and would have reached the summit by the time our people could get there. I told him that the next morning at daybreak 40 men with their muskets would be on shore and in readiness to march, and that I desired them to send me 40 Indians for the purpose of carrying their muskets and provisions.

The command of the expedition was given to Lieutenant Downes, and on the morning of October 29th, I gave the order to march. Gattanewa arrived at this moment and informed me that his daughter, who was married to a chief of the Happahs, had just descended the mountain and had come to beg for peace. From the old man's solicitude for peace, when contrasted with his former desire for war, I for a moment believed some treachery on foot. I had sent but a handful of men, and their arms, their ammunition, their provisions, and even their lives were in the hands of the Indians. Gattanewa was in my power, and I determined to secure him as a hostage until their return. I directed him to send for his daughter for the same purpose, but he informed me that she was far advanced in pregnancy and unable to come to the camp. I told him that no harm was intended, but that he must not leave the enclosure until the return of the party. The old man appeared very uneasy and repeatedly asked me if I would not kill him should any of our people be injured by the Happahs. My assurances to the contrary did not relieve his anxiety.

About eleven o'clock, we perceived our people had gained the mountains and were driving the Happahs from height to height. The Happahs fought as they retreated and dared our men to follow them with threatening gesticulations. A native who bore the American flag waved it in triumph as he skipped along the mountains— Lieutenant Downes and his men were attended by a large concourse of friendly natives, armed as usual, who generally kept in the rear. Mouina alone could be seen in the advance of the whole and was well known by his scarlet cloak and waving plumes. In about an hour, we lost sight of the combatants and saw no more of them until four o'clock, when they were discovered descending the mountains bearing five dead bodies slung on poles.

Mr. Downes and his men arrived soon afterward. He informed me that on his arrival near the tops of the mountains, the Happahs had assailed him and his men with spears and stones and that he had driven them from place to place until they had taken refuge in a fortress. Here they all made a stand, to the number of between 3,000 and 4,000. They dared our people to ascend the hill, at the foot of which they had made a halt to take breath. The word was given by Mr. Downes to rush up the hill, and at that instant a stone struck him in the belly and laid him breathless on the ground. At the same instant one of our people was pierced with a spear through his neck. This occasioned a halt, but Mr. Downes soon recovered and gave orders for a charge.

Hitherto, our party had done nothing. The Happahs had scoffed at our men and exposed their posteriors to them, treating them with the utmost contempt and derision. The friendly natives also began to think we were not as formidable as we pretended. It became, therefore, absolutely necessary that the fort should be taken at all hazards.

Our people gave three cheers and rushed on through a shower of spears and stones. It was not until our men entered the fort that the Happahs thought of retreating. Five were at this instant shot dead. One, in particular, fought until the muzzle of the piece was presented to his forehead, when the top of his head was entirely blown off. As soon as the fort was taken, all further resistance was at an end.

As soon as the party returned, I gave orders for the liberation of Gattanewa. His alarm had been great, and terror had taken such fast hold on his mind that he dared not look behind lest he perceive some danger in pursuit of him. He supposed us stronger than we really were and dreaded an ally so powerful. Previous to his departure, I informed him that I was now ready for a message from the Happahs, but the poor old man's fright would allow him to attend to nothing but his own safety.

The bodies of the five men, I was informed, were lying in the public square, where the natives were rejoicing over them. I had been told by Wilson on my arrival that the natives of this island were cannibals. Indeed, in conversing with Gattanewa on the subject, he did not hesitate to acknowledge that it was sometimes practiced by certain characters but with much pride and exultation added that none of his family, to the earliest period of their existence, were known to have eaten human flesh or to have tasted a hog which had died or been stolen. He said they sometimes eat their enemies.

Desirous of clearing up the matter in my own mind, I proceeded the day after the battle, with Wilson and a marine, to the house of Gattanewa to claim the dead bodies for burial. I found the house filled with women making the most dreadful lamentations and surrounded by a large concourse of male natives. On my appearance, there was a general shout of terror. I approached the wife of Gattanewa and required to know the cause of this alarm. She said that now we had destroyed the Happahs, they were fearful we should turn on them. She took hold of my hand, which she kissed and moistened with her tears. Then, placing my hand on her head, she knelt to kiss my feet. She told me they were willing to be our slaves—that their houses, their lands, their hogs, and all were ours—but begged that I would have mercy on her and her family and not put them to death. It seemed they had worked themselves up to the highest pitch of fear and could see in me nothing but the demon of destruction. I raised the poor old woman from her humble position and begged her to banish her groundless fears, saying that I had no intention of injuring any person residing in the valley of Tieuhoy. Addressing myself to her daughter, an interesting woman of about 23 who had come to solicit peace, I told her I would respect any messenger sent from her tribe bearing a white flag. I was now as ready to make peace as I had been to punish their insolence.

I was told Gattanewa was at the public square rejoicing over the bodies of the slain. I proceeded there and met the old man hastening home. He had been out from the earliest dawn and had not broken his fast. He held in one hand a coco shell containing a quantity of sour preparation of the breadfruit. In the other hand he had a raw fish, which he occasionally dipped into the preparation as he ate it. As soon, however, as Wilson gave him to understand that the practice of eating raw fish was disagreeable to me, he wrapped the remainder in a palm leaf and handed it to a youth to keep for him.

On my approach to the square, I could hear the natives beating their drums and chanting their war songs. I soon discovered 500 or 600 of them assembled about the dead bodies, which were lying on the ground still attached to the poles with which they had been brought from the scene of action. The warriors were all armed with spears, and several large drums, highly ornamented with cloth, were placed near the slain. Several priests, elevated above the rest, appeared to preside over the ceremonies. "Ah!" said Wilson, "they are now making their infernal feast on the bodies of the dead."

At the moment my approach was discovered, they were all thrown into the utmost confusion. The dead bodies were snatched from where they lay and hurried to a distance among the bushes. I now believed the truth of Wilson's declaration, and my blood recoiled with horror at the spectacle I was on the point of witnessing. I directed them in an authoritative manner to return the bodies to the place whence they had taken them.

With much reluctance they brought them back. Two of them were carefully covered with branches of the coco tree, and the others were entirely uncovered. To my great surprise, I found them unmutilated. I told them I had come to claim the bodies, that they might be buried, and that I was apprehensive that they intended to eat them. I expressed, with the strongest marks of horror, my detestation of the practice.

The Tayees assured me that they had no intention of eating the bodies but entreated that I would indulge them a day or two longer to perform their ceremonies and that I would grant them two to offer as a sacrifice to the manes of their priests, who had been slain. Being in some measure satisfied that these people were not cannibals, I consented to their keeping two on their promise that the others be sent to the camp.

I informed Gattanewa the ceremonies might proceed. The priest mounted on his elevation, and the warriors ranged themselves in lines about the square. The priest, after shaking the dried branch of a palm tree to which was hung a bunch of human hair, repeated a few words. Three shouts were given by the warriors, each shout accompanied by a loud clap of the hands, after which the drums beat for the space of about five minutes. All sang with loud voices and animated gestures until, their voices gradually dying away, silence ensued. This ceremony was three times performed and, at each time, with more and more animation. Wilson told me they were singing their victory over their enemies and returning thanks to their gods for sending me to their aid. After the ceremony was over, the priest asked me if it was not *motahee* (very fine). On my signifying my assent, it gave the most lively pleasure.

I now heard that one of the Happahs had arrived and directed for him to be sent for. He approached, trembling for his safety. On my offering my hand, which I had taught all the natives was a token of friendship, his fears seemed to subside. I learnt from him that many of the tribe were badly wounded and that the whole were in the utmost dismay and desired nothing more ardently than peace. I represented to him the folly of opposing their arms to ours and gave him a white handkerchief which was attached to a spear, informing him that the bearer of that should be respected.

The next day Mowattaeeh, a chief of the Happahs and son-in-law to Gattanewa, came and brought with him the white handkerchief which I had sent. I informed him that, as I had offered them peace and they had rejected it and put me to the trouble of chastising them, it was proper that we should receive some compensation. We were in want of hogs and fruit, and they had an abundance of them. I wished them to give me a supply once a week for my people, for which they should be compensated in iron and such other articles as would be most useful to them. Gattanewa and many of his tribe were present and appeared charmed with the terms offered to the Happahs.

After a short silence Mowattaeeh observed that we must suffer much from the rain in our tents, as they did not appear capable of securing us from the wet. "Yes," said Gattanewa, "and we are bound to make the *Hekai* (a title which they all gave me) and his people comfortable while they remain with us. Let every tribe at peace with him build a house for their accomodation, and the people of the valley of Tieuhoy will show them the example by building one for the residence of Opotee (the nearest they could come to the name Porter)." The proposal met with general applause, and people were immediately dispatched to prepare materials for erecting the fabric next day, at which time the Happahs promised to bring in their supply.

In the course of the day, the other chiefs of the Happahs came in with their flags and subscribed to the terms proposed. In less than two days I received envoys from every tribe on the island, with the exception only of the warlike tribes of Typees.

Agreeing to the request of the chiefs, I laid down the plan of the village about to be built. The line on which the houses were to be placed was already traced by our barrier of water casks. They were to take the form of a crescent, to be built on the outside of the enclosure, and to be connected with each other by a wall 12 feet in length and 4 feet in height. On the 3rd of November, upward of 4,000 natives from the different tribes assembled at the camp with materials for building. Before night, they had completed a dwelling house for myself and another for the officers, a sail loft, a cooper's shop, a place for our sick, a bakehouse, a guardhouse, and a shed for the sentinel to walk under. The whole was connected by walls. We removed our barrier of water casks and took possession of our village, which had been built as if by enchantment.

Nothing could exceed the regularity with which these

people carried on their work, without any chief to guide them, without confusion, and without much noise. Every man appeared to be master of his business, and every tribe appeared to strive which should complete their house with most expedition and in the most perfect manner. When the village was completed, I distributed among them several harpoons and, as usual, gave them an opportunity of contending for old iron hoops. All were perfectly happy and contented. It was the cause of great pleasure to Gattanewa and his people that I praised the house they had built above all the rest.

By the time our village was completed, everything had been taken out of the frigate and the powder and provisions deposited on board the prizes. The ship had been thoroughly smoked with charcoal to destroy the rats, which, on opening the hatches, were found in great numbers about the large pots in which the fires were made. Several tubs full of them were collected and thrown overboard, and it was supposed that, exclusive of the young which were killed in their nests and could not be found, we did not destroy a less number than from 1,200 to 1,500. The calking and other repairs of the ship went on with much expedition and regularity, and among other defects, we found our main-topmast in a very decayed state. We were, however, enabled to replace it with a spare one on board, and everything promised that we should not meet with many embarrassments or delays.

However, as soon as our painting commenced, we felt the want of oil. We caught two remarkably large sharks and endeavored to substitute the oil extracted from their livers, but found it would not answer. We next tried blackfish oil, but it did not succeed. Fortunately, having a small quantity of the oil of the black whale on board our prizes, we found it answered nearly as well to paint as that which is extracted from flaxseed and generally known by the name of linseed oil. With this we were enabled to improve the external appearance of the ship but had not a sufficient quantity to paint her inside. We afterward, however, found that this island affords an excellent substitute for linseed oil in the oily walnut, used by the natives for ripening bananas and for candles.

We found our copper much injured in many parts a little below the surface of the water. We were enabled, by means of the supply we had obtained and secured from our prizes, to make the necessary repairs after giving the ship a slight careen. Her bottom was found to have on it barnacles in considerable quantities, together with much grass and moss, which had no doubt collected at the Galápagos. To cleanse it and free the ship from those embarrassments, which must greatly impede her sailing, natives were employed, who, by diving down, and with the assistance of the outer shell of the coconut, soon removed them. The boatswain, as soon as he had completely overhauled the rigging of the ship, was employed on shore, with a number of hands, where a ropewalk was established. This was for the purpose of enlarging to a suitable size for a sea stock the whale line and other small cordage found on board our prizes, as also to make into small cordage the junk remaining from our old and condemned cables.

Everything went on with order and regularity. Every person was employed to the best advantage, and yet all were allowed sufficient time for amusement and relaxation. Wrestling, throwing the spear, jumping, and pitching quoits occupied some of their leisure time.

Some time after this, I sent a messenger to the Typees to inquire if they wished to be at peace with us. I told them I was willing to meet them on the same terms as the other tribes and only required an exchange of presents as a proof of their friendly disposition. In reply, they required to know why they should desire a friendship with us or why they should bring us hogs and fruit. If I was strong enough, they knew I should come and take them.

Their message was delivered to me in the presence of Gattanewa, Mouina, and many of the friendly tribes. Mouina frothed with rage and was for proceeding to hostilities immediately, but Gattanewa became serious and dejected. After a silence of a few minutes, he told me he would send his son to advise them to be friendly with us. "Nay," said the old man, "I will go myself. They are not aware of the dreadful effects of *bouhies*, and they must not suffer in consequence of their ignorance." I told him to send his son, that he was too old to proceed to so great a distance, and that I would wait until his return before I determined what course to pursue.

In two days the son returned and was desired by the Typees to tell Gattanewa and all the people of the valley of Tieuhoy that they were cowards—that we had beat the Happahs because the Happahs were cowards; that as to myself and my people, we were white lizards, mere dirt; that, as the most contemptible epithet they could apply, we were the posteriors and the privates of the Tayees. We were, they said, incapable of standing fatigue, overcome by the slightest heat and want of water, and could not climb the mountains without the Indians to assist us and carry our arms. Yet we talked of chastising the Typees, a tribe which had never been driven by an enemy and, as their gods informed them, were never to be beaten.

"Now," said Gattanewa, "I consent to war. They deserve chastisement." Mouina shortly afterward appeared at the village boiling with rage and, in a rather peremptory tone, insisted on immediate hostilities. I thought it necessary to check the manner of Mouina, lest it might become contagious and I should find a difficulty in keeping them in that subjugation by which, only, we could render ourselves secure. I told him, therefore, that I did not need his advice and that I should go to war or make peace when I thought proper without consulting him—that it was only necessary that he should do as I directed him. I further told him to leave our village until he could learn to conduct himself more respectfully.

Mouina walked off a few paces among the crowd, then, turning round, coolly said he believed I was a great coward. Forgetting that this was the observation of a mere Indian, I seized a musket and pursued him. He retreated among the crowd, and on my approaching him, presenting the musket, and threatening him with destruction on a repetition of such expressions, terror was marked on his countenance. I directed him immediately to leave the enclosure and never presume to enter it again.

Everything now bore the appearance of war; the Tayees and Happahs could talk and think of nothing else. Apprehensive, however, of a change of disposition on their part, I now conceived the design of constructing a fort, not only as a protection to our village and the harbor, but as a security to the Tayees against further invasion. But before the commencement of this undertaking, I considered it advisable to obtain the consent of the tribes of the valley. I had, for some time past, intended leaving my prizes here as the most suitable place to lay them up, and this fort would give them additional security. Besides, I believed that the possession of this island might at some future period be of importance to my country, and I was desirous of rendering her claim to it indisputable.

With these objects in view, I called on Gattanewa and inquired of him and his people, who had assembled, whether they had any objections to my constructing the fort. They informed me that they were much pleased with my intention, as it would enable me to give them more effectual protection, and requested that they might be permitted to assist in its construction. I now required to know of them whether they would always be faithful to the American flag and assist us in opposing our enemies. They replied that they had placed themselves entirely under my control and protection, that our enemies should be their enemies, and that they would always receive my countrymen as brethren among them. Gattanewa requested that they might not only be our friends and brothers, but also our countrymen. I promised them that they should be so and would be adopted as soon as the fort was completed.

Some short time prior to this, an event took place which threatened disagreeable consequences. The matter was, however, adjusted much to my satisfaction, and, on the whole, I considered the circumstance which gave rise to it as the most fortunate that could have happened. It relieved me entirely from my anxiety on a subject which, of all others, had given me the most uneasiness.

Robert Dunn, quartermaster, had been threatened by an officer of the watch with punishment for some neglect of duty. Dunn said that the time for which he enlisted had expired and if he was punished, he would never again do duty in the ship. Most of my crew were in the situation of Dunn. With as little loss of time as possible, I caused all hands to be called on the quarter-deck, where I informed them of the offense of Dunn. Then, directing him to strip, I assured him that I should punish him severely—to prevent his ever doing duty in the ship, I should turn him on shore on the island, as his time was out and it was proper that he should have his discharge.

Addressing myself to the ship's company, I expressed a determination to have no man under my command who had it in his power to say his time was out and he would no longer do duty. I informed them that the times of many were out and from that moment I gave up all claim on them for their services. They were their own masters and should have their discharge on the spot. If they wished to enlist again for the cruise, I would enlist them, give them the usual advance, and, on a suitable occasion, give them three days' liberty on shore. That such as refused to enlist but would bind themselves to do duty might remain on board till I could put them on shore in some civilized place. They should be supplied with provisions, but should be allowed neither pay nor prize money. Such as wished their discharge were called on for their names, in order that it might be made out in form. Shipping papers were laid open for all such as wished to enter.

I was now about proceeding to the punishment of Dunn, when most of the officers, petty officers, and seamen came forward and solicited his pardon, stating that he had appeared intoxicated at the time. Dunn also begged forgiveness most earnestly and hoped, whatever other punishment I might inflict, I would not turn him on shore. I thought it on the whole advisable to pardon him, and the men were dismissed. Every man of all the ships re-entered except one who, from some foolish whim, did not wish to re-enlist, although he was desirous of remaining, doing duty and receiving pay. I determined not to depart from the principles laid down. I stopped his pay and afterward sent him to America in the *New Zealander*.

On the 19th of November, the American flag was displayed from our fort and the following declaration read and signed, after which the prosperity of our newly acquired island was drunk by all present.

"It is hereby made known to the world that I, David Porter, a captain in the Navy of the United States of America and now in command of the United States frigate the *Essex*, have on the part of the United States taken possession of the island called by the natives Nooaheevah, but now called Madison's Island.

"That by the request and assistance of the friendly tribes residing in the valley of Tieuhoy, as well as of the tribes residing on the mountains whom we have conquered and rendered tributary to our flag, I have caused the village of Madison to be built, consisting of six convenient houses, a ropewalk, bakery, and other appurtenances, and for the protection of the same, as well as for that of the friendly natives, I have constructed a fort calculated for mounting 16 guns, whereon I have mounted four, and called the same Fort Madison.

"Our rights to this island, being founded on priority of discovery, conquest, and possession, cannot be disputed. But the natives, to secure to themselves that friendly protection which their defenseless situation so much required, have requested to be admitted into the great American family, whose pure republican policy approaches so near to their own. And in order to encourage these views to their own interest and happiness, as well as to render secure our claim to an island valuable on many considerations, I have taken on myself to promise them they shall be so adopted—that our chief shall be their chief. They have given assurances that such of their brethren as may hereafter visit them from the United States shall enjoy a welcome and hospitable reception among them and be furnished with whatever refreshments and supplies the island may afford. Also, that they will protect them against all their enemies and, as far as lies in their power, prevent the subjects of Great Britain from coming among them until peace shall take place between the two nations.

"Influenced by considerations of humanity, which promises speedy civilization to a race of men who enjoy every mental and bodily endowment which nature can bestow, as well as by views of policy, which secure to my country a fruitful and populous island possessing every advantage of security and supplies for vessels, I take possession of said island, called Madison's Island, for the use of the United States, whereof I am a citizen. The act of taking possession was announced by a salute of 17 guns from the artillery of Fort Madison and returned by the shipping in the harbor, which is hereafter to be called Massachusetts Bay.

"That our claim to this island may not be hereafter disputed, I have buried in a bottle, at the foot of the flagstaff in Fort Madison, a copy of this instrument together with several pieces of money, the coin of the United States.

"In witness whereof I have hereunto affixed my signature this 19th day of November, 1813.

"David Porter."

"THEY . . . BLEW THEIR WAR CONCHS FROM ONE END OF THE VALLEY TO THE OTHER."

The Tayees and the Happahs now made fresh complaints of the insults and aggressions of the Typees. Feeling that it was necessary to bring the Typees to terms or endanger his own good understanding with the other tribes and consequently the safety of his men, Porter attacked on November 28th.

The attack was launched from the Essex Junior *with the assistance of Tayee and Happah war canoes—a landing on the beach in the bay of the Typees. Porter, Downes, and a small force of 35 men were joined by approximately 5,000 warriors. Not a Typee was to be seen for a high and almost impenetrable swampy thicket reached to within 100 yards of the beach. The order to march was given, and the brave Mouina, having forgotten his differences with Porter, placed himself, as usual, in advance. The force had advanced about a mile into the bushes when they were suddenly assailed by*

*spears and stones from the unseen enemy. Lieutenant
Downes received a blow which broke his leg. Porter,
Lieutenant Gamble, and Dr. Hoffman found shelter
behind a fallen tree and thus were able to keep firing.
Theirs were the only muskets which could be employed
to any advantage. The sides of the mountains were
covered with warriors, for the natives began to desert
their friends and simply sat as silent observers. Even
Mouina began to hang back and begged for retreat
when Porter's force was reduced to 19 men.*

*It was only with extreme difficulty that Porter ex-
tricated himself and his men from this difficult situation,
and he returned to the beach with no contemptible
opinion of the enemy he had encountered. Unable to
draw that enemy out into a clear space, and disgusted
with bush fighting, Porter returned to Massachusetts
Bay with the* Essex Junior.

The behavior of the friendly natives, and particularly
the Happahs, convinced me I had now no alternative
but to prove our superiority by a successful attack upon
the Typees. It was obvious that the whole of the tribes
would join the conquering side, as is always the case
with savages. Accordingly, the next day, I determined to
proceed with a force which I believed they could not
resist. I selected 200 men from the *Essex,* the *Essex
Junior,* and the prizes. I directed boats to be prepared
to start with them before daylight next morning and
cautioned everyone to be secret as to my intentions, not
wishing to be annoyed by the confusion of the tribes
of Indians, whom we had always found useless to us.

In the evening, the boats became leaky and unable to
carry the men. As a consequence, I caused the party to
be sent on shore and determined to go by land. We had

a fine moonlight night, and I hoped to be down in the Typee [Taipi] valley long before daylight. Supposing we should be unaccompanied by many Indians, I calculated to take the Typees by surprise; we had guides who, we believed, could be depended upon for their knowledge of the road. I sent word of my intentions to Gattanewa, in order that neither he nor his people might be alarmed by our warlike movements, and directed the party sent in advance to halt, as soon as they had gained the top of the mountain, until I came up with the main body. There I intended encamping for the night, should our men not be able to stand the fatigue of a longer march. Several did give out before we reached the summit, which we did in about three hours with great difficulty. But after resting a short time and finding ourselves refreshed, the moon shining out bright, and our guides informing us (though very incorrectly) that we were not more than six miles from the enemy, we again marched.

Several Indians had joined us, but I had imposed silence on them as we were passing a Happah village. I was fearful of their discovering us and giving intelligence to the Typees. Not a whisper was heard from one end of the line to the other. Our guides marched in front, and we followed in silence up and down the steep sides of rocks and mountains, through riverlets, thickets, and reed brakes, and by the sides of precipices which sometimes caused us to shudder.

At twelve o'clock, we could hear the drums beating in the Typee village valley, accompanied by loud singing, and the number of lights in different parts of it induced me to believe they were rejoicing. I inquired the cause and was informed by the Indians they were celebrating their victory over us and calling on their gods to give them rain in order to render our *bouhies* useless. We soon arrived at the pathway leading from the top of the mountains into the valley. The Indians told us it would be impossible to descend it without daylight, that the mountain was almost perpendicular, that in many places we should be under the necessity of lowering ourselves down with great caution, and that it would even be necessary for them to assist us in the daytime to enable us to get down with safety. Believing from experience that when the natives considered the road bad it would really prove so to us, I concluded it advisable to wait for daylight before attempting to descend. We were on a narrow ridge running between the valleys of the Happahs and the Typees, well situated to guard against surprise and defend ourselves from an attack from either.

After placing guards, we laid down our arms. I had fallen into a doze when an Indian came to inform me it was coming on to rain very heavy and, as he expressed himself, would *"mattee! mattee! bouhie."* The rain caused loud shouts of joy in the Typee valley, and drums were beating in every quarter. From the violence of the rain, which soon poured down in torrents, I had little hope that a musket would be kept dry or a cartridge saved. Never in my life did I spend a more disagreeable night. A cold and piercing wind accompanied the deluge and chilled us to the heart. Without room to keep ourselves warm by moving about, fearful of stirring lest we might be precipitated into eternity down the steep sides of the mountains, as the ridge had become so slippery we could scarcely keep our feet, we all anxiously looked for morning. The first dawn of day, although the wind and rain still continued, was a cheering sight to us. We were all as perfectly wet as though we had been under water the whole time, and the Indians kept exclaiming that our muskets were spoiled and wished us to retreat in time. As soon as it was light, I went among my men to inquire into the state of their arms and ammunition. The first had escaped better than I had any reason to hope. Of the latter, more than one half was unfit for service.

When it was light enough to see down into the valley of the Typees, we were astonished at the greatness of the height we were above them and the steepness of the mountain by which we should have to descend to get to them. A narrow pathway pointed out the track, but it was soon lost among the cliffs. The Indians informed me that, in the present slippery state of the mountain, no one could descend. As our men were much harassed with fatigue, overcome with hunger, shivering, and uncomfortable, I determined to take up my quarters in the Happah valley on the opposite side of the mountain until the next day. I hoped by that time the weather would prove more favorable.

Before I left the hill, I directed my men to assemble on the ridge and to fire a volley to show the natives that our muskets had not received as much injury as they had expected. I believed, at that moment, the Happahs would not have hesitated in making an attack on us, and I thought it best to convince them we were still formidable. I had also other motives for firing. The Tayees and Happahs would accompany us into the Typee valley, and I thought it would be best to give the Typees timely notice of our approach, that they might remove their women and children, their hogs and most valuable effects. Although I felt it necessary to chastise them into submission, I wished to prevent the innocent from suffering and the pillage and destruction of their property. My own men, I knew, would be sufficiently occupied in fighting to prevent their plundering, but the Indians would be intent on that object alone.

The Typees had not, until this time, seen us, nor had they the least suspicion of our being there. As soon as they heard the report of our muskets and discovered our numbers, which, with the Indians of both tribes who had now assembled, was very numerous, they shouted, beat their drums, and blew their war conchs from one end of the valley to the other. And what with the squealing of the hogs, which they now began to catch, the screaming of the women and children, and the yelling of the men, the din was horrible.

We now descended with great difficulty into the village of the Happahs and were shown into the public square. We saw no appearance of cooking hogs, however, and no fruit was brought in. Nor did the natives appear disposed to accommodate us further than to abandon to us their houses. Everything was taken out of them, and we were left to shift for ourselves in the best manner we could. I requested a mat to sleep on, but it was long before it could be obtained. I wanted a piece of cloth to wrap around my loins while my clothes were washing and drying, and it was with great difficulty I could get it. The Happah warriors assembled about us, armed with their clubs and spears. The women, who had at first crowded around, now began to abandon us. Everything bore the appearance of a hostile disposition on the part of the Happahs. Our friends the Tayees cautioned us to be on our guard. I directed everyone to keep their arms in their hands, ready to assemble at a moment's warning.

I now sent for their chief and told him I expected his people to bring us hogs and fruit. I also directed that they should lay down their clubs and spears. No notice being taken of these demands, I caused many of their spears and clubs to be taken from them and broken. I sent parties out to shoot hogs, while others were employed in cutting down coconut and banana trees, as our people were too much fatigued to climb them to get the fruit. The chiefs and people of the Happah tribe now became intimidated and brought and baked hogs in greater abundance than was required. Friendship was re-established, and the women returned. When night approached, lookouts were placed and fires made before each house. Those of the tribe of Tayees remained with us. The Happahs retired.

At daylight next morning, we equally divided our ammunition, and the line of march was formed. All had put their arms in a good state for service, and all were fresh and vigorous, each being supplied with a small quantity of provisions for the day. On ascending the ridge where we had passed such a disagreeable night, we halted to take breath and view this delightful valley, which was soon to become a scene of desolation. It was about nine miles in length and three or four in breadth and surrounded on every part, except the beach, by lofty mountains. The upper part was bounded by a precipice of many hundred feet in height, from the top of which a handsome sheet of water was precipitated and formed a beautiful river which ran meandering through the valley and discharged itself at the beach. Villages were scattered here and there. Breadfruit and coconut trees flourished luxuriantly and in abundance. Plantations laid out in good order, enclosed with stone walls, were in a high state of cultivation, and everything bespoke industry, abundance, and happiness. Never in my life did I witness a more delightful scene or experience more repugnancy than I now felt for the necessity to make war against this happy and heroic people.

Many may censure my conduct as wanton and unjust, but let us reflect a moment on our particular situation. A handful of men residing among numerous warlike tribes, liable every moment to be attacked by them and cut off, our only hope of safety was in convincing them of our great superiority over them. From what we have already seen, we must either attack them or be attacked. Wars are not always just and are rarely free from excesses. However I may regret the harshness with which motives of self-preservation compelled me to treat these high-spirited and incorrigible people, my conscience acquits me of any injustice. Had no opposition been made, none would have been killed. Had they wished for peace, it would have been granted. But, proud of the honor of being the greatest warriors on the island, they believed themselves invincible and hoped to insult all others with impunity.

A large assemblage of Typee warriors were posted on the opposite banks of the river and dared us oppose them. In their rear was a fortified village secured by strong stone walls. Drums were beating and war conchs sounding. I gave orders to descend. Mouina offered himself as our guide, and I directed him to halt before crossing the river, to give time to the rear to close so all might rest. As soon as we reached the foot of the mountain, we were annoyed by a shower of stones from the bushes and from behind the stone walls. Being short of ammunition, I would not permit any person to fire. I directed the scouting parties to gain the opposite bank of the river and followed with the main body. Before all had crossed, the fortified village was taken without any loss on our side. Their chief warrior and another were killed and several wounded, but they retreated only to stone walls situated on higher ground. Three of my men were wounded and many of the Typees killed before we dislodged them; the spears and stones were flying from the bushes in every direction. We were satisfied, from the opposition made, that we should have to fight our way through the valley. Scouting parties were sent out in different directions to scour the woods, and another fort was taken after some resistance.

It now became necessary to guard against a useless consumption of ammunition. The scouting parties had returned, and some had expended all their cartridges. I forbade any firing from the main body unless we should be attacked by great numbers. I left a party posted in a house with the wounded, another party in ambush behind a wall, and directed Mouina to lead us to the next village. Before marching, I sent a messenger to inform the Typees that we should cease hostilities when they no longer made resistance, but so long as stones were thrown, I should destroy their villages. No notice was taken of this message.

We continued our march up the valley and met in our way several beautiful villages, which were set on fire, and at length arrived at their capital. We had been compelled to fight every inch of ground as we advanced, and here they made considerable opposition. The place was, however, soon carried, and I very reluctantly set fire to it. The beauty and regularity of the capital was such as to strike every spectator with astonishment. Their grand site, or public square, was far superior to any other we had met with. Numbers of their gods were here destroyed; several large and elegant new war canoes, which had never been used, were burned in the houses that sheltered them. Many of their drums, which they had been compelled to abandon, were thrown into the flames.

Our Indians loaded themselves with plunder after

destroying breadfruit and other trees and all the young plants they could find.

We had now arrived at the upper end of the valley, about nine miles from the beach and at the foot of the waterfall above mentioned. The day was advancing; we had much yet to do. It was necessary to hasten our return to the fort first taken, where we arrived after being about four hours absent, leaving behind us a scene of ruin and desolation. I had hoped that the Typees had now abandoned all further thoughts of resistance, but on my return to the fort, I found the parties left there had been annoyed the whole time in my absence. However, being sheltered from the stones and short of ammunition, they had not fired on the enemy.

This fort was situated exactly halfway up the valley. To return by the road by which we descended the hill would have been impossible. It therefore became necessary to go to the beach, where, I was informed, the difficulty of ascending the mountain would not be so great. Many were exhausted, and I ordered a halt, that all might rest and refresh themselves. After resting about half an hour, I directed the Indians to take care of our wounded. We formed the line of march and proceeded down the valley, in our route destroying several other villages, at all of which we had some skirmishing with the enemy. At one of those places, situated at the foot of a steep hill, they rolled enormous stones down with a view to crushing us to death. They did us no injury. The number of villages destroyed amounted to ten, and the plunder carried off by the Indians was great. The Typees fought us to the last and even, at first, harassed our rear on our return, but the parties left in ambush soon put a stop to any further annoyance.

We at length came to the formidable fort which

checked our career on our first day's enterprise, only two days previously. Although I had witnessed many instances of the ingenuity of these islanders, I never had supposed them capable of contriving and erecting a work like this, so well calculated for strength and defense. It formed the segment of a circle, about 50 yards in extent, built of large stones, six feet thick at the bottom and gradually narrowing at the top, to give it strength and durability. On the left was a narrow entrance merely sufficient to admit of one person's entering and serving as a sally port. But to enter this from outside, it was necessary to pass directly under the wall for one half its length, as an impenetrable thicket prevented the approach to it in any other direction. The wings and rear were equally guarded, and the right was flanked by another fortification of greater magnitude and equal strength and ingenuity. On viewing the strength of this place, I could not help felicitating myself on the lucky circumstance which had induced me to attack them by land, for I believed we should have failed in an attempt on this place.

I had determined, on first starting, not to return until I had destroyed this fort. To have thrown it down by removing the stones singly would have required more time than we had to spare. Concluding that by our united efforts we should be enabled to demolish the whole at once, I directed the Indians and my own men to put their shoulders to the wall and, by efforts made at the same time instant, to endeavor to throw it down. But it was built with so much solidity that no impression could be made on it. We therefore left it as a monument, to future generations, of their skill and industry. This fortification appeared of ancient date, and time alone can destroy it. We succeeded in making a small breach in the wall, through which we passed on our route to the beach, a route which was familiar to us but which had now become doubly intricate from the number of trees which had since been cut down and placed across our pathway, as much to impede our advance as to embarrass us in our retreat.

On my arrival at the beach, I was met by the chief of the Happahs, who invited me to return to their valley, assuring me that an abundance of everything was already provided for us. Gattanewa met me on the side of the hill as I was ascending to the Happah village. The old man's heart was full; he could not speak. He placed both my hands on his head, rested his forehead on my knees, and after a short pause, he raised himself and placed his hands on my breast, exclaiming, "Gattanewa," and then, "Opotee," to remind me we had exchanged names.

When I reached the summit of the mountain, I stopped to contemplate the valley which, in the morning, we had viewed in all its beauty, the scene of abundance and happiness. A long line of smoking ruins now marked our traces from one end to the other. The opposite hills were covered with the unhappy fugitives, and the whole presented a scene of desolation and horror.

We spent the night with the Happahs, who supplied us most abundantly. The next morning at daylight, we started for Madison's Ville, where we arrived about eight o'clock after an absence of three nights and two days, during which time we marched upward of 60 miles by paths which had never before been trodden but by the natives. Several of my stoutest men were for a long time laid up by sickness occasioned by their excessive fatigue, and one died two days after his return.

The day of our return was devoted to rest. A messenger, however, was dispatched to the Typees informing them that I was willing to make peace. He informed me on his return that the Typees were in the utmost consternation, but that my message had diffused the most lively joy among them. A flag of truce would be sent in next day to know my conditions. The Typee flag was borne by a chief accompanied by a priest, and I informed them that I still insisted on a compliance with the conditions formerly offered them—an exchange of presents and peace with myself and the tribes who had allied themselves to me. They readily consented to these terms and requested to know the number of hogs I should require, stating that they had lost but few and could supply us abundantly. I told them I should expect 400 and they would receive the customary presents in return. These, they assured me, would be delivered without delay.

Flags were now sent to me again from all tribes in the island with large presents of hogs and fruit. Our enclosure, though spacious, was not sufficient to contain the hogs we received; I therefore was under the necessity of sending them on board the different ships in as great numbers as could be kept there. Still, notwithstanding we killed pork on shore for our people every day, the number of hogs increased so fast that it became necessary to turn them out of the enclosure and let them run, which was done after marking them by cutting off the right ear and slitting the left. I informed the inhabitants of the valley of the mark I had put on them, in order that they might not kill them, but would feed and fatten them against my return. The number that I turned loose did not fall short of 500, my ships were all full, and a sufficient stock was reserved in the enclosure to supply us as long as we should remain here. I did not regret being overstocked.

Peace was now established throughout the island. The utmost harmony reigned, not only between us and the Indians, but between all the tribes. They mixed with one another in the most friendly manner, and the different priests came daily to visit me. They were all much delighted that they might now visit the different parts of the island in safety. Many of the oldest men assured me that they had never before been out of the valley in which they were born. I informed them that I should shortly leave them and return again at the expiration of a year. I exhorted them to remain at peace with one another and assured them that if they should be at war on my return, I should punish the tribes most at fault.

The chiefs, the priests, and the principal persons of the tribes affected to be solicitous of forming a relationship with me by an exchange of names with some of my family. Some wished to bear the name of my brother, my son-in-law, my son, my brother-in-law, and when all the male names were exhausted, they as anxiously solicited the names of the other sex. As many bore the names of the females of my family as of the males. The name of my son, however, was more desired than any other. Many old men whose long gray beards rendered their appearance venerable were known by the name of Pickineenee Opotee.

On the 9th of December, I had all my provisions, wood, and water on board, my decks filled with hogs, and a most abundant supply of coconuts and bananas. These we had been furnished by our Nooaheevan friends, who had reserved for us a stock of dried coconuts, suitable for taking to sea and calculated for keeping three or four months.

I now found it necessary to restrain the liberty I had heretofore given to my people. I directed that every person should remain on board and work late and early to hasten the departure of the ship. But Nooaheevah had many charms for a sailor. Three of my crew, determined to have a parting kiss, swam on shore at night and were caught on the beach and brought to me. I caused them to be confined in irons and determined to check any further disobedience of my orders by the most exemplary punishment. Next morning, I had them punished at the gangway and set them to work in chains with my prisoners. This severity excited some discontents and murmurings among the crew, but it effectually prevented a recurrence of this offense.

This affair, however, like to have ended seriously. My crew did not see the same motives for restraint as myself. They had long been indulged and thought it now hard to be deprived of their usual liberty. They were restless, discontented, and unhappy. The girls lined the beach from morning until night and every moment importuned me to take the taboos off the men, laughingly expressing their grief by dipping their fingers into the sea and touching their eyes so as to let the salt water trickle down their cheeks. Others would seize a chip and, holding it in the manner of a shark's tooth, declared they would cut themselves to pieces in despair. Some threatened to beat their brains out with a spear of grass, some to drown themselves, and all were determined to inflict on themselves some dreadful punishment if I did not permit their sweethearts to come on shore.

The men did not bear it with such good humor. Their situation, they said, was worse than slavery. One Robert White declared that the crew of the *Essex* had come to a resolution not to weigh anchor or, if they should be compelled to get the ship under way, to hoist their own flag in three days' time after leaving the port. When this was reported to me, it became necessary to notice it. With such a variety of characters as composes the crew of a ship at war, none but energetic measures will answer. I was willing to let them ease their minds with a little grumbling—it was no more than I expected. But a threat of this kind was carrying matters rather too far.

I called all hands on the larboard side of the quarter-deck. After stating to them the necessity of getting the ship in readiness for sea with all possible dispatch, I informed them that that was the sole cause of their confinement. I then represented the serious consequences which would be likely to result should all hands so far forget their duty to the service and their respect to my orders as to follow the example of those who were now under punishment for going on shore without leave.

I now informed them of the report which had been circulated and assured them that, although I gave no credit to it, should such an event take place I would, without hesitation, put a match to the magazine and blow them all to eternity. I added, "Perhaps there may be some grounds for the report. Let me see who are and who are not disposed to obey my orders. You who are inclined to get the ship under way, come on the starboard side, and you who are otherwise disposed, remain where you are." All hastened to the starboard side. I now called White. He advanced, trembling. I informed them this was the man who had circulated a report so injurious to the character of the crew, and indignation was marked on every countenance. An Indian canoe was paddling by the ship. I directed the fellow to get into her and never let me see his face again.

The prizes *Seringapatam, Sir Andrew Hammond,* and *Greenwich* were safely moored under the fort. They were placed in charge of Lieutenant Gamble of the marines, who, with Midshipman Feltus and 21 men, volunteered to remain with them until my return. In my orders to Lieutenant Gamble, I exhorted him to pay every regard to the most friendly intercourse with the natives and to endeavor to introduce among them the cultivation of seeds of different kinds. I left him with these vessels in order to secure the means of repairing my ships in case of an action on the coast. To avoid his being unnecessarily detained here, I instructed him to leave the island in five and a half months if he should not hear from me by then.

I also gave Mr. King orders to proceed to the United States with the *New Zealander*. All our letters, carefully put up in lead, were to be thrown overboard in case of capture. I prepared to sail with the *Essex* and the *Essex Junior* with a full supply of provisions, leaving an abundance for nine months on board the prizes. Prior to leaving the bay, I delivered orders to Mr. Downes. As it was not absolutely necessary that the two ships remain together, I made the best of my way regardless of the *Essex Junior*. But the ships sailed so near alike that we rarely lost sight of her for more than a few hours during several days together.

Shortly after our leaving port, a circumstance took place which caused me much sorrow. Tamaha, an Otaheitan [Tahitian] I had on board, received a blow from the boatswain's mate, the first, probably, he had ever received, as his gentle disposition and desire to give satisfaction had endeared him to everyone on the ship. Tamaha was ever lively and cheerful, constantly at work during working hours. Afterward, his chief employment was in amusing the crew by dancing after the manner of his country or in imitating the dancers of ours. He was with all a favorite. Tamaha could not bear the shame of a blow. He shed a torrent of tears and declared that no one should strike him again. We were about 20 miles from land, night was coming on, and it was blowing fresh with a considerable sea. Tamaha jumped overboard and was seen no more. His loss was greatly lamented by us all, and his melancholy fate caused a general dejection.

On the 3rd of February, I anchored in the bay of Valparaíso. I exchanged salutes with the battery, paid my respects to the governor, and, the next day, received his visit under a salute. The *Essex Junior* was directed to cruise off the port, to intercept the enemy's merchant vessels and to apprise me of the appearance of any of his ships of war. In the meantime, every effort was made to get the *Essex* ready for sea, while my crew were allowed by turns to go ashore on liberty.

Not having had an opportunity to return the hospitalities of the Chileans on my former visit, I took advantage of the present occasion to supply the omission. On the evening of the 7th, I invited the officers of the government, their families, and all the other respectable inhabitants to an entertainment on board the *Essex*. To give Lieutenant Downes an opportunity to participate in these gaieties, I directed him to anchor his vessel, but so as to have a full view of the sea.

The dancing continued until midnight, after which Lieutenant Downes repaired to his vessel, got her under way, and proceeded to sea. We had not yet taken down the awnings and flags which we employed for decorations, nor got clear of the confusion which so large a company naturally occasioned, before the *Essex Junior* made a signal for two enemy ships in sight. At this time, one half of my crew was on shore. Having established a signal for them to repair on board, I caused a gun to be fired and, after directing the ship to be prepared for action, repaired on board the *Essex Junior* and went out to reconnoiter. Both vessels had the appearance of frigates. I directed Lieutenant Downes to run into port and take a position where we could mutually defend each other.

On my return to the *Essex* at half past seven, only one hour and a half after the enemy came in sight, I found the ship completely prepared for action and every man on board and at his post. We had now only to act on the defensive. At eight o'clock, the two ships came into the harbor. The frigate, which proved to be the *Phoebe,* Captain Hillyar, ranged up alongside the *Essex* and between her and the *Essex Junior.* The *Phoebe* was fully prepared for action.

Captain Hillyar very politely inquired after my health, to which inquiry I returned the usual compliment. Finding the *Phoebe* was approaching nearer than prudence or a strict neutrality would justify me in permitting, I observed to Captain Hillyar that my ship was perfectly prepared for action but that I should only act on the defensive. He immediately answered me as he leaned over the quarter, in a careless and indifferent manner, "Oh, sir, I have no intention of getting on board of you." I told him again if he did fall on board of me there would be much bloodshed. He repeated his assurances, with the same nonchalance, that such was not his intention.

Finding, however, that he luffed up so as to cause his ship to take aback, whereby her jib boom came across my forecastle, I immediately called all hands to board the enemy, directing them, if the ships' hulls touched, to spring upon the deck of the *Phoebe.* At this moment, not a gun from the *Phoebe* could be brought to bear on either the *Essex* or the *Essex Junior,* while her bow was exposed to the raking fire of the one and her stern to that of the other. Her consort, which proved to be the *Cherub,* of 28 guns, was too far off to leeward to be of any assistance.

It is quite impossible for me to describe the consternation on board the *Phoebe* when they saw every officer and man of the *Essex* armed with a cutlass and a brace of pistols, ready to jump on board. They had been informed that the *Essex* was in great confusion from the entertainment and that the greater part of the crew was on shore. On witnessing this unexpected preparation for his reception, Captain Hillyar raised both hands and protested with the utmost vehemence that he had no intention of getting on board of me, that it was altogether an accident that his ship was taken aback, that he was exceedingly sorry she had been placed in that situation, and that he had no hostile intention in doing so.

The *Phoebe* was, at this moment, completely at my mercy. I could have destroyed her in 15 minutes. The temptation was great, and the equivocal appearance of this near approach of the enemy might have justified my attacking him on the plea of self-defense. But I was disarmed by these assurances of Captain Hillyar. I hailed Lieutenant Downes and told him not to commence any hostilities without my orders, as it was my intention to allow Captain Hillyar to extricate himself from his disagreeable situation. The *Phoebe* accordingly separated from the *Essex,* drifted by my ships, constantly exposed to their raking fire, and, after getting clear of them, anchored on the eastern side of the harbor within reach of her long 18-pounders but beyond the reach of my carronades. The *Cherub* anchored within pistol shot of my larboard bow, and I ordered the *Essex Junior* to take a position that would place the *Cherub* between her fire and that of the *Essex*—an arrangement that gave great umbrage to her commander, Captain Tucker.

On my going ashore, there was a general expression of astonishment among the officers of the government and the people of Valparaíso at my forbearance in not taking advantage of the opportunity which had thus presented itself for destroying the enemy. My reply was that I had always respected the neutrality of their port and should scrupulously continue to do so. Nor, although subsequent events have proved that Captain Hillyar was incapable of a similar forbearance, have I ever regretted for a single moment that I permitted him to escape when, either by accident or design, he placed himself entirely at my mercy.

The day after their arrival, Captain Hillyar and Captain Tucker paid me a visit at the house of Mr. Blanco, where I generally stayed while on shore. Their visit was soon returned and a friendly intimacy established, not only between the commanders and myself, but the officers and boats' crews of the respective ships. No one would have supposed us to have been at war, our conduct toward each other bore so much the appearance of a friendly alliance. At our first interview, I asked Captain Hillyar whether he intended to respect the neutrality of the port. He replied with much emphasis and earnestness: "You have paid so much respect to the neutrality of the port that I feel myself bound in honor to respect it." I told him the assurance was sufficient and that it would place me more at ease, since I should now no longer feel it necessary to be always prepared for action.

In the course of this conversation, I adverted to a flag he had hoisted containing the following motto: "God and country; British sailors' best rights; traitors offend both." I asked him the object of it. He said it was in reply to my motto of "Free trade and sailors' rights," which gave great offense to the British Navy. Whenever I hoisted that flag, he should not fail to hoist the other. I told him my flag was intended solely for the purpose of pleasing ourselves and not to insult the feelings of others—that his, on the contrary, was considered as highly insulting in the light of an offset against ours. If he continued to hoist it, I should not fail to retort on him.

The next day, his flag being hoisted, I displayed one

bearing the motto "God, our country, and liberty—tyrants offend them." The thing was taken in good part by Captain Hillyar. We talked freely and good-humoredly of the object of his coming to that sea, the long hunt he had after me, and of my views in coming to Valparaíso. He asked me what I intended to do with my prizes and when I was going to sea. I told him whenever he should send the *Cherub* away, I should go to sea, but it would depend on him altogether when I departed—that having thus met him, I should seek an opportunity of testing the force of the two ships. I added that, the *Essex* being smaller than the *Phoebe,* I did not feel I should be justified to my country for losing my ship if I gave him a challenge. But if he would challenge me and send away the *Cherub,* I would have no hesitation in fighting him.

To these and similar observations, Captain Hillyar replied that the results of naval actions were very uncertain and depended on many contingencies—the loss of a mast or spar often turned the fate of the day. He observed that, notwithstanding the inferiority of my ship, still, if I could come to close quarters, I could do great damage with her carronades. On the whole, he would trust to circumstances to bring us together, as he was not disposed to yield the advantage of a superior force which would effectively blockade me until other ships arrived. At all events, it would prevent my doing any further injury to the commerce of Britain.

As regarded my prizes, I informed him they were only encumbrances to me and I should take them to sea and destroy them at the first opportunity. He told me I dared not do it while he was in sight. I replied, "We shall see."

Finding Captain Hillyar determined to yield none of

the advantages of his superior force, and being informed there were other ships bound into the Pacific Ocean in pursuit of me, I secretly resolved to take every means of provoking him to a contest with his single ship. The *Cherub* being quite near the *Essex,* the respective crews occasionally amused themselves with singing songs, selecting those most appropriate to their situation and feelings. The songs from the *Cherub* were better sung, but those from the *Essex* were more witty and to the point. The national tune of "Yankee Doodle" was the vehicle through which the crew of the *Essex,* in full chorus, conveyed their nautical sarcasms. The "Sweet Little Cherub That Sits up There" was usually selected by their rivals. These things were not only tolerated but encouraged by the officers through the whole of the calm, delightful nights of Chili, much to the amusement of the people of Valparaíso. At length Captain Hillyar requested me to put a stop to this practice. I informed him I certainly should not do so while the singing continued on board the *Cherub.*

About this time I thought it advisable to know the sailing of my ship and that of the enemy. I therefore chose a favorable opportunity, when the British vessels were to leeward and unable to cut me off, to get under way and let them chase me. I soon ascertained the *Essex* had greatly the advantage and consequently believed I could, at almost any time, make my escape from them. I did not like, however, to abandon the hope of bringing the *Phoebe* to action. Notwithstanding my own impatience to depart, I determined to keep it under control while I endeavored to provoke my adversary to combat.

On the afternoon of February 25th, it being calm and the two British ships far in the offing, I towed one of my prizes, the *Hector,* to sea. When within reach of their guns, I set fire to her and made my escape from them, notwithstanding every effort on their part to cut me off. This insult had the desired effect. On the 27th, the *Cherub* was about two or three miles to leeward of the port and the *Phoebe* was seen standing in for the harbor. At five o'clock, she hove about, a short distance from me, with her head off shore, shortened sail, fired a gun to windward, and hoisted the flag containing the motto intended as an answer to mine. As every man on board my ship considered this a challenge, I did not hesitate a moment to accept of it as such. I immediately hoisted my motto, fired a gun, and got under way. The *Phoebe* now stood off shore and made sail. I followed her, increased sail, and was closing with her very fast when, to my astonishment, she bore up before the wind and ran down for her consort. My indignation was roused at this conduct, and I directed two shot to be fired ahead of her to bring her to, but she continued on her course. I consequently hauled my wind and returned into port. When the *Phoebe* had joined her consort, both gave chase to me. After I had anchored, they came gallantly into the harbor together.

I confess I felt exceedingly indignant at this conduct of Captain Hillyar and so expressed myself on shore among the inhabitants. Certain of these expressions were communicated to the British residents in Valparaíso and by them to Captain Hillyar. On the 16th of March, 12 days before my capture, the first lieutenant of the *Phoebe* came on board the *Essex* under a flag of truce and stated that he had a message from Captain Hillyar. Presuming it was another challenge, I required the presence of some of my officers, to which he consented. He stated that Captain Hillyar had been informed that I had said he acted in a cowardly manner by running away from the *Essex* after challenging her, but could not believe the report and had sent him on board to ascertain the truth. I told him I had said so and still thought so.

He then stated that Captain Hillyar had entrusted him to tell me that his firing a gun and hoisting the flag was not intended as a challenge, but as a signal to the *Cherub*. I replied that Captain Hillyar had informed me the motto of the flag was intended for my ship and that there was not a man, woman, or child in Valparaíso that did not think it a challenge. He still repeated that Captain Hillyar had desired him to assure me it was not a challenge. I told him in reply that I had considered it one, but was bound to believe Captain Hillyar if he said it was not. I added that, however it might be intended, I should always consider it a challenge whenever he chose to send away the *Cherub* and, under that impression, act precisely as I had done before. Again, the officer assured me of the mistake, adding that Captain Hillyar was a religious man and did not approve of sending challenges.

These are the important circumstances which preceded the capture of the *Essex* in the bay of Valparaíso.

"MY SHIP WAS CUT UP IN A MANNER . . . NEVER BEFORE WITNESSED."

Captain Hillyar, according to Porter, seemed determined to avoid a contest with him on nearly equal terms. The two British ships were kept close together, for no action was to be risked unless both could engage the Essex.

Apprehensive that British reinforcements might arrive any day, Porter determined to run the blockade with the Essex. *His main object in leaving was to avoid the* Tagus, *rated 38 guns, and two other frigates that had sailed for the Pacific in pursuit of him. The* Raccoon *was also expected from the northwest coast of America, where she had been sent to destroy our fur establishments on the Columbia river. A rendezvous was appointed with the* Essex Junior *and every arrangement made for sailing. It was Porter's intention to let the enemy chase him off the coast, to give the* Essex Junior *a chance to escape.*

On the 28th of March, the day after this determination

was formed, the wind began to blow fresh from the southward, and the Essex *parted her larboard cable and dragged the starboard anchor directly to sea. It was the beginning of the end.*

Farragut, writing years later in his journal, gave his own version of the momentous events of that day and the tense days immediately preceding the battle:

"We arrived off the coast of Chili and ran down to Valparaíso, where we lay until the arrival of the British frigate *Phoebe* and sloop of war *Cherub.*

"When they made their appearance off the port, our whole watch, being a third of our crew, were on shore on liberty. The mate of an English merchantman which was lying in port at the time went immediately on board the *Phoebe* and stated to Captain Hillyar that one half of our men were on shore and that the *Essex* would fall an easy prey.

"The two ships then hauled into the harbor on a wind. The *Phoebe* made our larboard quarter, but the *Cherub* fell to leeward about half a mile. On gaining our quarter, the *Phoebe* put her helm down and luffed up on our starboard bow, coming within 10 or 15 feet of the *Essex.*

"As soon as the enemy hove in sight, we had fired a gun and hoisted a cornet for all men and boats to return. In 15 minutes every man was at his quarters, and but one was under the influence of liquor, he a mere boy. When the *Phoebe* was close alongside and all hands at quarters (the powder boys stationed with slow matches ready to discharge the guns—the boarders, cutlass in hand, standing by to board in the smoke, as was our custom at close quarters), the intoxicated youth saw, or imagined he saw, through the port, someone on the *Phoebe* grinning at him.

" 'My fine fellow, I'll stop your making faces,' he exclaimed, and was just about to fire his gun when Lieutenant McKnight saw the movement and with a blow sprawled him on the deck. Had that gun been fired, I am convinced the *Phoebe* would have been ours.

"We were all at quarters and cleared for action, waiting with breathless anxiety for the command from Captain Porter to board, when the English captain appeared, standing on the after gun in a pea jacket, and in plain hearing said, 'Captain Hillyar's compliments to Captain Porter, and hopes he is well.'

"Porter replied, 'Very well, I thank you. But I hope you will not come too near for fear some accident might take place which would be disagreeable to you,' and with a wave of his trumpet, the kedge anchors went up to our yardarms, ready to grapple with the enemy. Captain Hillyar braced back his yards and remarked to Porter that if he did fall aboard him, he begged to assure the captain it would be entirely accidental.

" 'Well,' said Porter, 'you have no business where you are. If you touch a rope-yard of this ship, I shall board instantly.' He then hailed the *Essex Junior* and told Captain Downes to be prepared to repel the enemy. But our desire for a fight was not yet to be gratified. The *Phoebe* backed down, her yards passed over ours not touching a rope, and she anchored about half a mile astern. We thus lost an opportunity of taking her, though we had observed the strict neutrality of the port under very aggravating circumstances.

"We remained together in the harbor for some days, when the British vessels, having completed their provisioning and watering, went to sea and commenced a regular blockade of our ships. One night we manned all our boats for the purpose of boarding the enemy outside.

The captain in his boat, with muffled oars, pulled so close up to the *Phoebe* that he could hear the conversation of the men on her forecastle, and thereby learned that they were lying at their quarters, prepared for us. The attempt was given up and we returned on board.

"It was understood in our ship one day that Captain Porter had sent word to Captain Hillyar that, if he would send the *Cherub* to the leeward point of the harbor, he would go out and fight him. We all believed the terms would be accepted, and everything was kept in readiness to get under way. Soon after, the *Phoebe* was seen standing in with her motto flag flying, 'God and our country! British sailors' best rights.' This was in answer to Porter's flag, 'Free trade and sailors' rights.' She fired a gun to windward, and the *Cherub* was seen running to leeward.

"In five minutes, our anchor was up, and, under topsails and jib, we cleared for action—in fact, we were always ready for that. Within two miles of our position, the *Phoebe* bore up and set her studding sails. However, as Captain Hillyar subsequently proved himself a brave man in more than one instance, I shall not deny him that common characteristic of a naval officer, and have attributed his action on these two occasions to a want of good faith. He was dealing with a far inferior force, and it was ignoble in the extreme on his part not to meet his foe when he had the ghost of an excuse for doing so, ship to ship.

"On the 28th of March, it came on to blow from the south, and we parted our larboard cable, dragging the starboard anchor leeward. We immediately got under way and made sail on the ship. The enemy's vessels were close in with the weathermost point of the bay, but Captain Porter thought we could weather them, so we hauled up for that purpose and took in our topgallant sails, which had been set over close-reefed topsails. Scarcely had the topgallant sails been clewed down when a squall struck the ship and, though the topsail halyards were let go, the yards jammed and would not come down. When the ship was nearly gunwale under, the main-topmast went by the board, carrying the men who were on the main-topgallant yard into the sea, and they were drowned. We immediately wore ship and attempted to regain the harbor but, owing to the disaster, were unable to do so. We anchored in a small bay, about a quarter of a mile off shore and three quarters of a mile from a small battery. But it was evident, from the preparations being made by the enemy, that he intended to attack us. We made arrangements to receive him as well as we possibly could. Springs were got on our cables, and the ship was perfectly prepared for action.

"I well remember the feeling of awe produced in me by the approach of the hostile ships—even to my young mind it was perceptible in the faces of those around me, as clearly as possible, that our case was hopeless. It was equally apparent that all were ready to die at their guns rather than surrender. There had been so much bantering between the men of the ships through letters and songs, with an invariable fight between the boats' crews when they met on shore, that a very hostile sentiment was engendered. Our flags were flying from every mast, and the enemy's vessels displayed their ensigns, jacks, and motto flags as they bore down grandly to the attack.

"At 3:54 P.M., they commenced firing, the *Phoebe* under our stern and the *Cherub* on our starboard bow. But the latter, finding out pretty soon that we had too many guns bearing on her, likewise ran under our stern. We succeeded in getting three long guns out of the stern ports and kept up as well-directed a fire as possible in such an unequal contest.

"In half an hour, they were both compelled to haul off to repair damages. During this period of the fight, we had succeeded three times in getting springs in our cables, but in each instance they were shot away as soon as they were hauled taut. Notwithstanding the incessant firing from both of the enemy's ships, we had, so far, suffered less than might have been expected, considering that we could bring but three guns to oppose two broadsides. We had many men killed in the first five or ten minutes of their fire, before we could bring our stern guns to bear.

"The enemy soon repaired damages and renewed the attack. Both ships took position on our larboard quarter, out of reach of our carronades and where the stern guns could not be brought to bear. They kept up a most galling fire, which we were powerless to return. The captain ordered the cable to be cut, and, after many ineffectual attempts, we succeeded in getting sail on the ship, having found that the flying-jib halyards were in a condition to hoist that sail. It was the only serviceable rope that had not been shot away. By this means we were enabled to close with the enemy, and the firing now became fearful on both sides.

"The *Cherub* was compelled to haul out and never came into close action again, though she lay off and used her long guns greatly to our discomfort, making a perfect target of us. The *Phoebe* was enabled, by the better condition of her sails, to choose her own distance suitable for her long guns and kept up a most destructive fire on our helpless ship. Captain Porter, finding it impossible to close with the *Phoebe,* determined to run his ship ashore and destroy her. Accordingly, we stood for the land, but when we were within half a mile of the bluffs, the wind suddenly shifted, took us flat aback, and payed our head off shore. We were again exposed to a galling fire from the *Phoebe*.

"Captain Downes of the *Essex Junior* came on board to receive his orders, being under the impression that our ship would soon be captured. His vessel was in no condition to be of service to us.

"Captain Porter ordered a hawser to be bent on to the sheet anchor and let go. This brought our ship's head around, and we were in hopes the *Phoebe* would drift out of gunshot, as the sea was nearly calm. But the hawser broke, and we were again at the mercy of the enemy. The ship was now reported to be on fire, and the men came rushing up from below, many with their clothes burning, which were torn from them as quickly as possible. Those for whom this could not be done were told to jump overboard and quench the flames. Many of the crew, and even some of the officers, hearing the order to jump overboard, took it for granted that the fire had reached the magazine and that the ship was about to blow up. They leaped into the water and attempted to reach the shore, about three quarters of a mile distant, in which effort a number were drowned.

"The captain sent for the commissioned officers, to consult with them as to the propriety of further resistance, but first went below to ascertain the quantity of powder in the magazine. On his return to the deck he met Lieutenant McKnight, the only commissioned officer left on duty, all the others having been either killed or wounded. It was evident the ship was in a sinking condition. It was determined to surrender in order to save the wounded. At 6:30 P.M., the painful order was given to haul down the colors.

"During the action I was like 'Paddy in the catharpins,' a man on occasions. I performed the duties of captain's aide, quarter gunner, powder boy, in fact did everything that was required of me.

"I shall never forget the horrid impression made upon me at the sight of the first man I had ever seen killed. He was a boatswain's mate and was fearfully mutilated. It staggered and sickened me at first, but they soon began to fall around me so fast that it all appeared like a dream and produced no effect on my nerves.

"I can remember well that, while I was standing near the captain, just abaft the mainmast, a shot came through the waterways and glanced upward, killing four men who were standing by the side of the gun. It took the last one in the head and scattered his brains over both of us. But this awful sight did not affect me half as much as the death of the first poor fellow. I neither thought nor noticed anything but the working of the guns.

"On one occasion Midshipman Isaacs came up to the captain and reported that a quarter gunner named Roach had deserted his post. The only reply of the captain, addressed to me, was, 'Do your duty, sir.' I seized a pistol and went in pursuit of the fellow but still did not find him. It appeared that when the ship was reported to be on fire, he had contrived to get into the only boat that could be kept afloat and had escaped with six others to the shore.

"The most remarkable part of this affair was that Roach had always been a leading man in the ship. On the occasion previously mentioned, when the *Phoebe* seemed about to run into us in the harbor of Valparaíso and the boarders were called away, I distinctly remember this man standing in an exposed position on the cathead, with sleeves rolled up and cutlass in hand, ready to board, his countenance expressing eagerness for the fight—which goes to prove that personal courage is a very peculiar virtue. Roach was brave with a prospect of success, but a coward in adversity.

"Soon after this, some gun-primers were wanted and I was sent after them. In going below, while I was on the wardroom ladder, the captain of the gun directly opposite the hatchway was struck full in the face by an 18-pound shot and fell back on me. We tumbled down the hatch together. I struck on my head, and, fortunately, he fell on my hips. He was a man of at least 200 pounds' weight, and I would have been crushed to death if he had fallen directly across my body. I lay for some moments stunned by the blow but soon recovered conciousness enough to rush up on deck.

"The captain, seeing me covered with blood, asked if I was wounded. To which I replied, 'I believe not, sir.' " 'Then,' said he, 'where are the primers?' This brought me completely to my senses, and I ran below again and carried the primers on deck. When I came up the second time, I saw the captain fall and, in my turn, ran up and asked if he was wounded. He answered me in almost the same words.

" 'I believe not, my son, but I felt a blow on the top of my head.' He must have been knocked down by the windage of a passing shot, as his hat was somewhat damaged.

"When my services were not required for other purposes, I generally assisted in working a gun—would run and bring powder from the boys and send them back for more—until the captain wanted me to carry a message.

"When it was determined to surrender, the captain sent me to ascertain if Mr. —— had the signal book and if so, to throw it overboard. I could not find him or the book for some time, but at last saw the latter lying on the sill of a port and dashed it into the sea. After the action, Mr. —— said he was overboard himself, trying to clear the book from some part of the wreck where it had lodged—a very unfortunate story, as I had seen it sink into the depths below. Isaacs and I amused ourselves throwing overboard pistols and other small arms to prevent their falling into the hands of the enemy.

"At length the boarding officer came on board and, running up to Captain Porter, asked him how he would account to somebody (I do not remember who) for allowing his men to jump overboard. At the same time he demanded his sword.

" 'That, sir,' replied Porter, 'is reserved for your master.' The captain went on board the *Phoebe,* and I followed half an hour later."

So ends Farragut's recollection of that fateful day. Captain Porter's official report of the battle to the Secretary of the Navy is as follows:

The *Phoebe,* agreeably to my expectations, came to seek me at Valparaíso, where I was anchored with the *Essex,* my armed prize the *Essex Junior,* under the command of Lieutenant Downes, on the lookout off the harbor. But, contrary to the course I thought he would pursue, Commodore Hillyar brought with him the *Cherub,* sloop of war, mounting 28 guns, eighteen 32-pound carronades, eight 24's, and two long 9's on the quarter-deck and forecastle, and a complement of 180 men. The force of the *Phoebe* is as follows: 30 long 18-pounders, sixteen 32-pound carronades, one howitzer, and six 3-pounders in the tops, in all, 53 guns and a complement of 320 men. This made a force of 81 guns and 500 men, in addition to which they took on board the crew of an English letter of marque lying in port. Both ships had picked crews and were sent into the Pacific for the express purpose of seeking the *Essex*.

The force of the *Essex* was 46 guns, forty 32-pound carronades, and six long 12's, and her crew, which had been much reduced by prizes, amounted to only 255 men. The *Essex Junior,* which was intended chiefly as a store ship, mounted 20 guns, ten 18-pound carronades, and ten short 6's, with only 60 men on board.

On the 28th of March, the wind came on to blow hard from the southward, when I parted my larboard cable and dragged my starboard anchor directly out to sea. Not a moment was to be lost in getting sail on the ship. The enemy were close in with the point forming the west side of the bay. I saw a prospect of passing to windward when I took in my topgallant sails, which were set over single-reefed topsails, and braced up for this purpose. But on my rounding the point, a heavy squall struck the ship and carried away her main-topmast, precipitating the men who were aloft into the sea, and they were drowned.

Both ships now gave chase to me, and I endeavored, in my disabled state, to regain the port. Finding I could not recover the common anchorage, I ran close into a small bay, about three quarters of a mile to leeward of the battery on the east side of the harbor. I let go my anchor within pistol shot of the shore, where I intended to repair my damages as soon as possible. The enemy continued to approach, showing an evident intention of attacking us regardless of the place where I was anchored. The caution observed in their approach to the attack of the crippled *Essex* was truly ridiculous, as was their display of their motto flags and the number of jacks at their mastheads. I, with as much expedition as circumstances would admit, got my ship ready for action and endeavored to get a spring on my cable but had not succeeded when the enemy, at 54 minutes after 3 P.M., made his attack.

The *Phoebe* placed herself under my stern and the *Cherub* on my starboard bow. But the *Cherub,* soon finding her situation a hot one, bore up and ran under my stern also, where both ships kept up a hot raking fire. I had got three long 12-pounders out at the stern ports, which were worked with so much bravery and skill that in half an hour we so disabled both as to compel them to haul off to repair damages. In the course of this firing, I had, by the great exertions of Mr. Edward Barnewell, the acting sailing master, assisted by the boatswain, succeeded in getting springs on our cables three different times—but the fire of the enemy was so excessive that before we could get our broadside to bear, they were shot away and thus rendered useless to us. My ship had received many injuries, and several men had been killed and wounded. But my brave officers and men, notwithstanding the unfavorable circumstances under which we were brought to action and the powerful force opposed to us, were nowise discouraged—all appeared determined to defend their ship to the last extremity and to die in preference to a shameful surrender. Our gaff, with the ensign and motto flag at the mizzen, had been shot away, but "Free trade and sailors' rights" continued to fly at the fore. Our ensign was replaced by another, and, to guard against a similar event, an ensign was made fast in the mizzen rigging and several jacks were hoisted in different parts of the ship.

The enemy soon repaired his damages for a fresh attack. He now placed himself with both his ships on my starboard quarter, out of the reach of my carronades and where my stern guns could not be brought to bear. He there kept up a most galling fire which it was out of my power to return, when I saw no prospect of injuring him without getting under way and becoming the assailant. My topsail sheets and halyards were all shot away, as well as the jib and fore-topmast staysail halyards. The only rope not cut was the flying-jib halyard. That being the only sail I could set, I caused it to be hoisted, my cable to be cut, and ran down on both ships with an intention of laying the *Phoebe* on board.

The firing on both sides was now tremendous. I had let fall my fore-topsail and foresail, but the want of tacks and sheets had rendered them almost useless to us. Yet we were enabled, for a short time, to close with the enemy. Although our decks were now strewed with the dead and our cockpit filled with the wounded, although our ship had been several times on fire and was rendered a perfect wreck, we were still encouraged to hope to save her, from the circumstance of the *Cherub* being compelled to haul off. She did not return to close action again, although she apparently had it in her power to do so, but kept up a distant firing with her long guns. The *Phoebe,* from our disabled state, was enabled by edging off to choose the distance which best suited her long guns and kept up a tremendous fire on us, which mowed down my brave companions by the dozen. Many of my guns had been rendered useless by the enemy's shot, and many of them had their whole crews destroyed. We manned them again from those guns that were disabled. One gun, in particular, was three times manned—15 men were slain at it in action, but, strange as it may appear, the captain of it escaped with only a slight wound.

Finding that the enemy had it in his power to choose

his distance, I now gave up all hopes of closing with him. As the wind, for the moment, seemed to favor the design, I determined to endeavor to run her on shore, land my men, and destroy her. Everything seemed to favor my wishes. We had approached the shore within musket shot, and I had no doubt of succeeding, when, in an instant, the wind shifted from the land (as is very common in this port in the latter part of the day) and payed our head down on the *Phoebe,* where we were again exposed to a dreadful raking fire. My ship was now totally unmanageable. Yet, as her head was toward the enemy and he to leeward of me, I still hoped to be able to board him.

At this moment, Lieutenant Downes came on board to receive my orders, under the impression that I would soon be a prisoner. He could be of no use to me in the then wretched state of the *Essex.* Finding (from the enemy's putting his helm up) that my last attempt at boarding did not succeed, I directed him, after he had been about ten minutes on board, to return to his own ship to be prepared for defending and destroying her in case of an attack. He took with him several of our wounded, leaving three of his boat's crew on board to make room for them. The slaughter on board my ship had now become horrible, the enemy continuing to rake us and we unable to bring a gun to bear. I therefore directed a hawser to be bent to the sheet anchor and the anchor to be cut from the bows to bring her head around. This succeeded. We again got our broadside to bear, and, as the enemy was much crippled and unable to hold his own, I have no doubt he would soon have drifted out of gunshot before he discovered we had anchored, had not the hawser unfortunately parted.

My ship had taken fire several times during the action,

but alarmingly so forward and aft. At this moment, the flames were bursting up each hatchway, and no hopes were entertained of saving her. Our distance from the shore did not exceed three quarters of a mile, and I hoped many of my brave crew would be able to save themselves, should the ship blow up. I was informed the fire was near the magazine, and the explosion of a large quantity of powder below served to increase the horror of our situation. Our boats were destroyed by the enemy's shot. I therefore directed those who could swim to jump overboard and endeavor to gain the shore. Some reached it. Some were taken by the enemy, and some perished in the attempt. But most preferred sharing with me the fate of the ship.

We who remained now turned our attention wholly to extinguishing the flames. When we had succeeded, we again went to our guns, where the firing was kept up for some minutes. But the crew had by this time become so weakened that they all declared to me the impossibility of making further resistance and entreated me to surrender my ship to save the wounded, as all further attempt at opposition must prove ineffectual, with almost every gun being disabled by the destruction of their crews.

I now sent for the officers of divisions to consult them, but what was my surprise to find only Acting Lieutenant Stephen Decatur McKnight remaining, who confirmed the report respecting the condition of the guns on the gun-deck. Those on the spar deck were not in a better state. Lieutenant Wilmer, after fighting most gallantly throughout the action, had been knocked overboard by a splinter while getting the sheet anchor from the bows and was drowned. Acting Lieutenant John Cowell had lost a leg. Mr. Edward Barnewell, acting sailing master, had been carried below after receiving two wounds, one in the breast and one in the face. Acting Lieutenant William Odenheimer had been knocked overboard from the quarter an instant before and did not regain the ship until after the surrender.

I was informed that the cockpit, the steerage, the wardroom, and the berth-deck could contain no more wounded—that the wounded were killed while the surgeons were dressing them and that, unless something was speedily done to prevent it, the ship would soon sink from the number of shot holes in her bottom. On my sending for the carpenter, he informed me that all his crew had been killed or wounded and that he had been once over the side to stop the leaks, when his slings had been shot away and it was with difficulty that he was saved from drowning.

The enemy, from the smoothness of the water and the impossibility of our reaching him with our carronades, and the little apprehension that was excited by our fire, which had now become much slackened, was enabled to take aim at us as at a target. His shot never missed our hull, and my ship was cut up in a manner which was, perhaps, never before witnessed. In fine, I saw no hopes of saving her and, at 20 minutes past 6 P.M., gave the painful order to strike the colors.

Seventy-five men, including officers, were all that remained of my whole crew, after the action, capable of doing duty. Many of them were severely wounded. Some have since died. The enemy still continued his fire, and my brave, though unfortunate, companions were still falling about me. I directed an opposite gun to be fired to show them we intended no further resistance, but they did not desist. Four men were killed at my side and others in different parts of the ship. I now believed he intended to show us no quarter and that it would be as well to die with my flag flying as struck. I was on the point of again hoisting it when, ten minutes after my hauling the colors down, he ceased firing!

I cannot speak in sufficiently high terms of the conduct of those engaged, for such an unparalleled length of time and under such circumstances, with me in the arduous and unequal contest. Let it suffice to say that more bravery, skill, patriotism, and zeal were never displayed on any occasion. Everyone seemed determined to die in defense of their much-loved country's cause, and nothing but views to humanity could ever have reconciled them to the surrender of the ship. They remembered their wounded and helpless shipmates below.

To Acting Lieutenants McKnight and Odenheimer I feel much indebted for their great exertions and bravery, throughout the action, in fighting and encouraging the men at their divisions, for the dexterous management of the long guns, and for their promptness in remanning their guns as their crews were slaughtered. The conduct of that brave and heroic officer, Acting Lieutenant John Cowell, who lost his leg in the latter part of the action, excited the admiration of every man in the ship. After being wounded, he would not consent to be taken below until loss of blood rendered him insensible. Mr. Edward Barnewell, acting sailing master, whose activity and courage were equally conspicuous, returned on deck after his first wound and remained, after receiving his second, until fainting with loss of blood. Mr. Samuel Johnson, who had joined me the day before and acted as marine officer, conducted himself with great bravery and exerted himself in assisting at the long guns, the musketry after the first half hour being useless from our great distance.

Mr. M. W. Bostwick, whom I had appointed acting purser of the *Essex Junior* and who was on board my ship, did the duties of aide in a manner which reflects on him the highest honor. And Midshipmen Isaacs, Farragut, and Ogden, as well as Acting Midshipmen Terry, Lyman, and Duzenbury and Master's Mate William Pierce, exerted themselves in the performance of their respective duties and gave an earnest of their value to the service. The three first are too young to recommend for promotion.

We have been unfortunate but not disgraced. The defense of the *Essex* has not been less honorable to her officers and crew than the capture of an equal force. I consider my situation less unpleasant than that of Commodore Hillyar, who, in violation of every principle of honor and generosity and regardless of the rights of nations, attacked the *Essex* in her crippled state within pistol shot of a neutral shore, when for six weeks I had daily offered him fair and honorable combat on terms greatly to his advantage. The blood of the slain must be on his head. He has yet to reconcile his conduct to heaven, to his conscience, and to the world.

Epilogue

"I . . . CONSIDER MYSELF . . . AT LIBERTY TO
EFFECT MY ESCAPE IF I CAN."

There are other reports of the conflict between the *Essex* and the *Phoebe;* the following is from two Chilean eye-witnesses:

"Among the few ships that stirred the waters of that deserted bay, there stood out imposingly, under the command of that gallant captain David Porter, the beautiful *Essex,* whose gay crew and no less gay officers in the hills of Valparaíso gave the sleepy town a holiday aspect. But like all good things, it could not last long.

"When in the midst of the gaiety which the presence of the *Essex* had caused, it was with dread that at the mouth of the bay were discerned, approaching in search of the *Essex,* the *Phoebe* and the *Cherub.* Under full sail, they sought to close to within gun range of the enemy.

"Shots were fired from land at the agressors to demonstrate to them how far out maritime jurisdiction extended. The intention of maintaining our neutrality therein was evidently understood by the English, for that day and the following one, they limited themselves to simply tacking beyond the range of the cannons.

"For 40 days the ships spied constantly upon each other. Every night from their decks the Yankees would sing 'Yankee Doodle' and the English would reply with 'God Save the King.' Later, insults and threats would be exchanged. By day, the threats would be made by signals.

"I recall the afternoon of March 28, when the officers of the *Essex,* who had come ashore in search of fresh provisions, were emptying bottles at the home of the Rosales family. Suddenly, the roar of a cannon from the *Essex* made them dash for their caps, and with no more leave-taking than a fantastic 'Good-by forever,' they leapt into their boats, shouting hurrahs, and pulled hurriedly out to their happy and confident ship.

"Many families rushed to the hills the better to witness what they surmised would come to pass. We saw the *Essex,* taking advantage of a slight breeze and confident in its greater speed, attempt to force the blockade. She must at all cost avoid the disaster of such an unequal engagement. The English ships, however, fearful lest this coveted prize should elude them, attacked it inside the neutral harbor. The breeze failed the *Essex* at the second tack, which forced her into such an unprotected position that we believed her aground. Here, in spite of the firing from our fortresses in defense of our neutral rights, the gallant *Essex* was destroyed on our very shores."

"The defense of the *Essex,*" Captain James Hillyar wrote into his report just after the battle at Valparaíso, "taking into consideration our superiority of force, the very discouraging circumstance of her having lost her main-topmast and being twice on fire, did honor to her brave defenders and most fully evinced the courage of Captain Porter and those under his command. Her colors were not struck until the loss in killed and wounded was so awfully great, and her shattered condition so seriously bad, as to render further resistance unavailing." According to the British captain, the fighting only became desperate during the last forty-five minutes of battle.

Porter, however, did not agree with Hillyar's official version of the fight. "I am informed," he wrote, "Commodore Hillyar has thought proper to state to his government that the action lasted only forty-five minutes. Should he have done so, the motive may be easily discovered. But the thousands of disinterested witnesses who covered the surrounding hills can testify that we fought his ships near two hours and a half. Upward of fifty broadsides were fired by the enemy, and upward of seventy-five by us. Except the few minutes they were repairing damages, the firing was incessant."

There is one unanswered question about that bloody day off the shores of Valparaíso. What was the *Essex Junior* doing during the battle? According to both Porter and Farragut, Lieutenant Downes came aboard the *Essex* to receive orders only when the situation was desperate and the ship in a sinking state. We can only conjecture that Downes was given verbal orders by his captain not to engage in the fight. This would seem likely, particularly since the *Cherub* withdrew to repair her own damages, and Downes may have been instructed to follow her in such circumstances. This theory gains some support from a memorandum Captain Porter wrote to

Downes in January, while both ships were sailing toward Valparaíso:

"Should I fall in with the *Phoebe,* the *Raccoon,* and *Cherub* all together, I shall endeavor to make my retreat in the best manner I can, and to effect this we must endeavor to help together and act from circumstances.

"If we fall in with the *Phoebe* and one sloop of war, you must endeavor to draw the sloop off in chase of you and get her as far to leeward of the frigate as possible, and as soon as you effect this, I shall engage the frigate.

"If we meet the *Phoebe* alone and to leeward of us, I shall run alongside of her. You must remain out of gunshot to windward of us until you see how matters are likely to go with us. If you find we can master her ourselves, you will not bring your ship into action but keep her free from injury to assist us in case of need. If you find, from the loss of our masts or other damage, that we are worsted, you will take a position that will most annoy the enemy, to enable us to haul off or take such advantage as may offer.

"If I should make the *Phoebe* to windward, I shall maneuver so as to endeavor to get the weather gauge; otherwise, I shall avoid coming fairly alongside of her, unless I can so disable her with my stern chase guns as to obtain an advantage.

"Should we make the *Phoebe* and a sloop to windward, draw the sloop off if you can and leave the *Phoebe* to me.

"I wish you to avoid an engagement with a sloop if possible, as your ship is too weak. If, however, you cannot avoid an action, endeavor to cut her up so as to prevent her coming to the assistance of the *Phoebe.*

"I shall, in all probability, run alongside of the *Phoebe*

under the Spanish pennant and ensign. Should I do so, you will show British colors until I hoist the American."

There were many instances of personal heroism during that March 28. Boatswain's Mate Kingsbury, who had come on board the *Essex* with Lieutenant Downes to "share the fate of his old ship," was so badly burned that "scarcely a square inch of his body escaped." Yet he swam to shore, and although he was deranged for some days, he ultimately recovered and lived to serve with Farragut in the West Indies.

Farragut writes in his journal that many of the crew bled to death for want of tourniquets. He tells of one young Scotsman with a leg shot off close to the groin who, using his handkerchief as a tourniquet, said to his comrades: "I left my own country and adopted the United States to fight for her. I hope I have this day proved myself worthy of the country of my adoption. I am no longer of any use to you or to her, so good-by." With these words he leaned on the sill of the port and threw himself overboard.

Another seaman who lost a leg during the action discovered the quarter gunner named Roach lurking on the berth-deck. Seizing a gun, the wounded seaman dragged his shattered stump after him as he tried to get a shot at Roach.

Young Lieutenant Cowell, one of Midshipman Farragut's best friends, lost a leg just above the knee. When the doctor proposed to drop another patient and attend to him, he refused with the words: "One man's life is as dear as another's; I would not cheat any poor fellow out of his turn." He died an hour later.

Out of the *Essex*'s complement of 255 men, 155 were killed, wounded, or missing after the action. Of these,

58 were counted dead. Captain Hillyar, on the other hand, reported only five killed and ten wounded on his two ships. Among the killed was William Ingram, first lieutenant of the *Phoebe,* who had previously visited the *Essex* under a flag of truce. Farragut relates that "his frank and manly bearing quite won the hearts of all on board." He also adds that he heard later that Ingram begged Captain Hillyar to bear down on the *Essex* and board her, for he thought it deliberate murder to lie off at long range and fire at the ship as though she were a target. The older man responded that he had gained his reputation by single-ship combats and he expected to retain it—to capture the *Essex* with the least possible risk to his vessel and crew.

Porter, younger and of a more ardent and impetuous temperament, was understandably outraged. The American captain told the English commodore, several days after the battle, in exceedingly plain language what he thought of the manner in which the *Essex* had been attacked. According to Porter, the tears came into Hillyar's eyes and, grasping the young man's hand, he said: "My dear Porter, you know not the responsibility that hung over me with respect to your ship. Perhaps my life depended on my taking her."

About eight o'clock the morning after the battle, Farragut relates, he went on board the *Phoebe* and was ushered into the steerage.

"I was so mortified at our capture that I could not refrain from tears. While in this uncomfortable state, I was aroused by hearing a young reefer call out: 'A prize! A prize! Ho, boys, a fine grunter, by Jove!'

"I saw at once that he had under his arm a pet pig,

belonging to our ship, called Murphy. I claimed the animal as my own.

" 'Ah,' said he, 'but you are a prisoner and your pig also.'

" 'We always respect private property,' I replied, and as I had seized hold of Murphy, I determined not to let go unless compelled by superior force. This was fun for the oldsters, who immediately sang out:

" 'Go it, my little Yankee! If you can thrash Shorty, you shall have your pig.'

" 'Agreed!' said I.

"A ring was formed in the open space, and at it we went. I soon found that my antagonist's pugilistic education did not come up to mine. In fact, he was no match for me and was compelled to give up the pig. So I took Master Murphy under my arm, feeling that I had, in some degree, wiped out the disgrace of our defeat.

"I was sent for by Captain Hillyar to come into his cabin, where Captain Porter was, and asked to take some breakfast, when, seeing my discomfiture, he remarked in a very kind manner:

" 'Never mind, my little fellow, it will be your turn next, perhaps.'

"I said I hoped so and left the cabin to hide my emotion."

After the battle, both the *Essex* and the *Phoebe* were in a sinking state, and it was with difficulty they could be kept afloat until anchored in Valparaíso the next morning. The masts and yards of the *Phoebe* and *Cherub* were badly crippled and their hulls cut up. The former had eighteen 12-pound shot through her, below her waterline, and nothing but the smoothness of the water, according to Porter, saved both the *Phoebe* and the *Essex*.

After being completely overhauled, the *Essex* sailed for England as the *Phoebe*'s prize and arrived in Plymouth Sound on November 13, 1814. In 1833, she was mentioned as a convict ship at Jamaica, and in 1837, she was sold at auction by order of the British Admiralty. There is no trace of her in subsequent records.

Soon after Porter's capture, he entered into an agreement with Commodore Hillyar to disarm his prize, the *Essex Junior,* and proceed with the survivors to the United States. Meantime, he was allowed to go on shore on parole with his officers and wounded crew members. The rest of the crew were placed under guard on board a Spanish merchant ship hired by the British. During this interval, young Farragut volunteered to "aid our surgeon as an assistant, and I never earned Uncle Sam's money so faithfully as I did during that hospital service. I rose at daylight and arranged the bandages and plasters until 8 A.M. Then, after breakfast, I went to work at my patients."

The ladies of Valparaíso took it upon themselves to care for the American wounded and were most kind. "Without their aid," Porter wrote, "I have no doubt many would have died who now live to thank them. For myself, I shall never forget their gentle humanity, and if it should not be in my power to return it, I bequeath the remembrance as a legacy of gratitude to be repaid by my country."

Neither Porter nor Mr. Poinsett, the consul general, had such charitable feelings toward the Chilean government, however. "When I commanded the most powerful force in the Pacific," Porter states, "all were willing to serve me. But when Captain Hillyar appeared with one still stronger, it became the great object to conciliate his friendship by evincing hostility to me." During the action, Poinsett had called on the government at Valparaíso for the protection of the port batteries for the *Essex*. This request was rejected, although the governor promised that if the *Essex* could return to the original anchorage, he would require a cease fire of Hillyar. Soon after the battle, Mr. Poinsett resigned his post in protest against this inaction and left the country.

On April 27, the *Essex Junior* left Valparaíso, having been converted into a cartel ship for carrying all the prisoners under parole to an American port. She was armed only with a passport given by Captain Hillyar to Porter, which requested all in authority under the British government to allow the ship to pass freely to the United States. Captain Porter, Lieutenant Downes, the rest of the officers, and the crew agreed to remain on board on parole and not to take arms against Great Britain until their exchanges as prisoners could be arranged by the governments of the two countries.

One hundred and thirty prisoners were on board—all that were left of Porter's men with the exception of Lieutenant McKnight, Midshipman Lyman, Mr. Adams, and eleven seamen. These three officers and eleven men had been exchanged already for a part of the crew of the captured British whaler *Sir Andrew Hammond*, which had been left by Porter at Nuku Hiva with Lieutenant Gamble. The men were not allowed to go home on the *Essex Junior* but were required to get their own passage on merchant vessels.

Mr. Adams apparently accompanied Captain Hillyar to England aboard the *Phoebe*. Lieutenant McKnight and Midshipman Lyman were required by Porter's agreement with Captain Hillyar to go to Rio de Janeiro, and to England, if necessary, to give evidence regarding the capture of the ship. It is presumed they went to Rio aboard the *Phoebe*. From Rio, the two men were allowed to proceed homeward and did so by the first available vessel, a Swedish ship sailing for England, where they hoped to obtain passage immediately for America. In mid-ocean, the men transferred to the United States Navy sloop *Wasp* and were never seen again. The *Wasp* is supposed to have been shipwrecked and was lost at sea.

Favored by good weather, the *Essex Junior* passed Cape Horn under topgallant studding sails and arrived off Sandy Hook in seventy-three days. There, however, she fell in with the *Saturn,* a British sloop of war commanded by a Captain Nash, and was searched and detained. Porter expressed astonishment at such proceedings and insisted that the smallest detention was a violation of both the contract he had signed with Captain Hillyar and the latter's passport requesting that the ship "be permitted to pass freely to the United States without any impediments." He declared he was no longer on parole and said he would consider himself a prisoner of Captain Nash. He offered his sword to the boarding officer, who refused to accept it. The boarding officer returned to the *Saturn* but was soon back with orders from Captain Nash that the *Essex Junior* was to remain all night under the lee of the *Saturn.*

"Tell Captain Nash," Porter said to the officer, "that if British officers have no respect for the honor of each other, I shall have none for them and shall consider myself, if detained all night, at liberty to effect my escape if I can." It was Porter's belief that Captain Nash had violated the passport. He therefore felt no obligation to remain on parole as a prisoner but considered himself free to fight again for his country.

At seven o'clock the next morning, when the ships were about thirty or forty miles off the eastern part of Long Island, Porter ordered his whaleboat manned, armed, and lowered and left the following message with Lieutenant Downes for Captain Nash: ". . . that Captain Porter was now satisfied that most British officers were not only destitute of honor but regardless of the honor of each other. That he was armed and prepared to defend himself against Captain Nash's boats if sent in pursuit of him. That he must be met, if met at all, as an enemy."

Porter kept the *Essex Junior* in a direct line between his whaleboat and the *Saturn* and had gotten nearly gunshot length from her before he was discovered. The *Saturn* instantly made all sail after the whaleboat, but a thick fog came on and Porter was hidden from view. He changed his course and effected his escape. Meantime, Lieutenant Downes also took advantage of the fog and the *Saturn*'s preoccupation with the escaping whaleboat. As Farragut tells the story:

"Making all sail ourselves for Sandy Hook, we were in a few minutes going about nine knots. At 11 A.M., the man from our royal masthead discovered the broad pennant of the *Saturn* to windward, and before she was out of the fog, we were all snug, with our main topsail to the mast. Firing a gun to leeward, she ran down to us and sent a boat alongside with another officer in charge. The first one who boarded us had conducted himself like a gentleman, but this individual was an upstart. He began by remarking:

" 'You drift quite fast; we have been going nine knots for the last three hours, and yet we find you abeam with your main topsail to the mast.'

" 'Yes,' was the quiet reply of Captain Downes.

" 'And that was Captain Porter who left the ship in a boat, I suppose?'

" 'It was,' said Downes.

" 'Then by G——d, you will soon be leaving, too, if we don't take your boats from you.'

" 'You had better try that,' Downes remarked coolly.

" 'I would, if I had my way,' replied the officer.

"Captain Downes' anger was now fully aroused, and, advancing, he said, 'You impertinent puppy, if you have any business to do here, do it. But if you dare to insult me again, I shall throw you overboard,' accompanying his words with a significant gesture.

"The young man jumped into his boat and left the ship. A short time after, the regular boarding officer came to us and stated that Captain Nash 'hoped Captain Downes would excuse the youth and ignorance of the former officer, who had been ordered to send an apology for his ungentlemanly conduct.' "

The *Essex Junior* was finally dismissed after being detained the whole day. She made all sail for Sandy Hook, where she arrived about 8 P.M. that evening. Downes took the ship in by chart and, when opposite a small battery, hoisted his colors and sent a boat on shore with a light in her. The light was accidentally extinguished, and the battery began firing on the boat, which continued until another light could be procured. Farragut remarks that the ship was not struck by a single shot, which made him think "it was not such an awful thing as was supposed, to lie under a battery."

"Having finally convinced them that we were Americans," Farragut continues, "we furled sails and remained all night, which was probably very fortunate, for the next morning as we stood into the harbor under full sail, with colors flying, a second battery opened up on us. So we found it almost as difficult to get rid of our friends as our foes."

The *Essex Junior* came to anchor at New York on July 7, 1814. Through his contract with Hillyar, Porter had arranged to have her purchased for the United States for $25,000, but she was seized by the marshal of the district and was condemned and sold in August for $8,100, according to Navy records. Lieutenant Downes, much to his surprise, had arrived home before Captain Porter, who, it turned out, was farther from land than he supposed when he left the *Essex Junior*.

After rowing and sailing about sixty miles, Porter landed, with great difficulty, through the surf near the town of Babylon, Long Island. Strongly suspected of being a British officer, he was closely interrogated and finally compelled to produce his commission to satisfy his questioners. The people of Babylon then gave him three cheers and a salute of twenty-one guns from a small swivel cannon. They hauled his boat from the water and placed it on an oxcart to go to New York. They also gave him a horse to ride, and at 5 P.M. the next day, he launched his boat again at Brooklyn for Manhattan. When it became known in the city that Captain Porter had arrived, a crowd took the horses from his carriage and, amid the shouts of the whole city, hauled him to his lodgings.

Early in August the officers and crew of the *Essex* were discharged from their paroles by order of the Secretary of the Navy and the Commissary General of Prisoners. Captain Nash's conduct had left them "as free to serve, in any capacity, as if they had never been made prisoners."

Meantime, in the Marquesas, where, on December 13,

1813, Porter had left Lieutenant Gamble with three officers, twenty men, six prisoners, and the prizes *Greenwich, New Zealander, Seringapatam,* and *Sir Andrew Hammond.* Gamble was having more than his share of troubles with sickness, native unrest, squalls, the rainy season, bad equipment, and desertions. The Tahitian Tamaha reappeared, and his story was almost incredible. He said he had become intoxicated and fallen overboard from the *Essex* about twenty miles from land. He had been drawn under the frigate and bruised in several parts of his body. After remaining in the water for one day and two nights, he managed to regain the shore. He had been picked up by a friendly Typee, who took him into his home to nurse him. Tamaha was aboard the *New Zealander* when she sailed for the United States with a full cargo of oil on December 26. The ship was retaken by a British cruiser just outside New York, and Tamaha was claimed as a subject of Great Britain and presumably sailed under her flag.

In short order, at Nuku Hiva, where the prizes were anchored, there followed: intertribal warfare; Gattanewa's illness, in which he suffered delusions that the Happahs had a lock of his hair and were killing him; nightly invasions of the ships by female natives; and a shortage of swine and vegetables. All this led to the mounting of additional guns at Fort Madison.

On the fourth of May, Gamble was informed by one of his seamen that his men were planning to mutiny. About the same time, he learned that Wilson, the interpreter, had reported among the natives that Opotee would not return and that the Americans intended to depart in a few days with two of the vessels then at anchor in the bay. Mutiny occurred on board the *Seringapatam* three days later. Gamble and Midshipmen Feltus and Clapp were tied and thrust into a small room on the ship, directly under the cabin floor. Robert White, the man whom Porter had expelled from the *Essex*, spiked the guns at the fort and on the other ships, unmoored the *Seringapatam*, and stood out of the bay. Later that evening, Gamble was wounded, and he and five others were turned out in an open boat to fend for themselves. They managed to return to the *Greenwich*, and Gamble now made plans to sail as soon as possible in the *Sir Andrew Hammond*.

Wilson, it turned out, was one of the principal instigators of their troubles. When a party of six loyal men was sent ashore to find him, four were massacred by the natives and the other two barely escaped with their lives. Setting the *Greenwich* on fire, the survivors cut the cables of the *Sir Andrew Hammond* and sailed in a leaky ship without a boat or anchor to help her in distress. Gamble's crew was now reduced to seven men and himself, of whom only two were in good health and fit for duty.

After stopping off at the Hawaiian Islands, Gamble was captured on June 13 by Captain Tucker of the *Cherub*. It was here that he heard for the first time of the loss of his old ship. The *Cherub* arrived at Valparaíso on September 23 and Rio de Janeiro on October 28, where Lieutenant Gamble waited for a ship on which he could book passage home. Finally, after an absence of two years and ten months, the marine lieutenant reached his native land on August 27, 1815.

Madison's Island, or Nuku Hiva, did not become a United States possession, for the American government never ratified Porter's claim. France took possession of the islands in 1842.

Almost a year to the day before Lieutenant Gamble's

arrival in New York, Captain Porter issued the following call to his old crew:

"Free Trade and Sailors' Rights
"To the crew of the old *Essex:* Sailors, the enemy is about attempting the destruction of your new ship at Washington, and I am ordered to defend her. I shall proceed immediately, and all disposed to accompany me will meet me at three o'clock this afternoon at the navy agent's office. New York. August 22, 1814."

On his return home, Porter had been offered the command of the *Columbia,* of forty-four guns, then being built at Washington. The name of the vessel was subsequently changed to *Essex.* The enemy at that time had entered the Potomac and were marching on Washington. On August 22, their armies were only twenty miles from the capital.

Porter, busy collecting his men, was not able to reach Washington until the British were already evacuating the city. He erected a battery about thirty miles below the city, along the Potomac. Then, as the British ships sailed down the river, he fired on them. There had not been sufficient time to get the heavy guns into position, however, and the enemy managed to return the fire, pass the battery, and sail home with their plunder. Nonetheless, they were badly battered, while the Americans lost only eleven killed and nineteen wounded. Among the property that was destroyed by the British at this time was the new *Essex* at the Navy Yard.

Lieutenant Downes, not long after his arrival home, was promoted to the rank of captain and later sailed on the *Macedonian* and *Java.* His last sea duty was in command of the frigate *Potomac*. Eventually, he became commandant of the Boston Navy Yard.

David Glasgow Farragut lived to become the naval hero of the Civil War. In 1866, he became an admiral, a rank especially created for him by Congress.

Captain Porter next commanded the *Fulton,* an experimental war steamer, and in 1815 he was appointed a commissioner of the Navy Board. Eight years later, he resigned this post to go to sea once more—as commander in chief of a squadron to suppress piracy in the West Indies.

He was so successful that two years later, when he turned the job over to his successor, piracy in the area was almost at an end. During that time, however, one of his officers landed at Puerto Rico in pursuit of a pirate and was imprisoned by local Spanish authorities. Porter, without reporting the matter or waiting for instructions, seized a Puerto Rican fort in retaliation and demanded an apology. For this hostile action against a friendly power, Porter was recalled by the Navy, court-martialed, and suspended for six months. He resigned his commission in the Navy as a result.

In 1826, Porter went to Mexico, which was then in revolt against Spain, and accepted the post of commander in chief of the Mexican navy. He returned home three years later, discouraged by a year of enforced inaction at Vera Cruz. He had been intrigued against by the Mexican officials, his assassination had been twice attempted, and he had lost both a son and a nephew, who had served under him.

Porter was anxious to go back to Mexico as a United States official, to settle with his enemies, but there was no vacancy in that ministry. His friend Andrew Jackson offered him a post in the Navy, which he declined, still smarting from his court-martial. Finally, he was appointed consul general at Algiers and the next year became chargé d'affaires at Constantinople. He died in 1843 while filling the post of minister to Constantinople.

Impetuous, rash, and headstrong, Porter was also courageous, firm, and just. He had a natural talent for handling ships and men. He loved his country but was sometimes too ready to see abuses against her honor. His main fault, if it is one, was his tendency to act too independently and on his own authority. In retrospect, it seems a minor fault in the light of the services he rendered his country.

As a legacy, he gave to America two of its most illustrious naval officers, David G. Farragut, his adopted son, and David Dixon Porter, his son, who served with Farragut and followed him as Admiral of the United States Navy.

Glossary

About—A ship is said to be going about when in the act of tacking or changing directions

Armorer—A man in charge of the repair and maintenance of small arms

Athwart—Across

Baffle—To beat back or hinder

Ballast—A quantity, usually of iron, stone, or gravel, placed in the hold to give a ship proper stability when she has little or no cargo

Barracuda—A voracious pikelike fish

Bend—To make fast

Berth-deck—The deck where the men slept

Blockade—To close off from traffic or communication by naval force

Blunderbuss—A short gun with large bore and flaring mouth

Boatswain—The officer who has charge of the cordage, boats, and rigging

Boom—A spar for spreading the foot of a sail

Bow—The front of a ship

Bowsprit—A spar projecting forward beyond the front, or stem, of a ship on which various jibs and staysails are set

Bowsprit, to fish—To apply a large piece of wood to a bowsprit to strengthen it

Breadfruit—Edible fruit of breadfruit tree. Large, round, starchy mass that, when baked, resembles fresh bread.

Brig—Short for brigantine, a two-masted ship, square-rigged on both masts

Broadside—A discharge of all guns on one side of a ship, both above and below

Burden—The carrying capacity of a vessel

Cable—A large rope by which a ship is secured to its anchor

Canvas—Strong cloth of which sails are made

Carronade—A short chambered piece of ordnance of large caliber and short range

Cartel—A written agreement between governments for the exchange of prisoners

Casaba—A muskmelon

Catharpins—Short ropes used to keep the lower shrouds or large ropes tight, to permit sharp bracing of the lower yards

Cathead—A large piece of timber projecting over the bow for drawing up the anchor clear of a ship's side

Chains—A ledge built out on the side of a ship, where the shrouds are fastened

Cleats—Pieces of wood to fasten ropes to

Clew—The lower corner of a square sail. The after lower corner of a fore-and-aft sail. Clew lines are ropes that come down from the yards to the lower corners of the sail and by which the clews of the sails are hauled up or lowered.

Cockpit—An apartment for the wounded in a warship

Colors—The flag of the nation under which a ship sails. To strike the colors is to lower the flag in token of submission.

Conch—A large spiral marine shell

Cooper—One who makes or mends casks or barrels

Cordage—Ropes and cords collectively

Cornet—A flag or standard, specifically, a signaling flag

Corvette—A warship equipped with sails and a single tier of guns, ranking next below a frigate

Courses—Sails bent to the lower yards of any square-rigged vessel

Coxswain—The person who steers a boat

Cutlass—A short swordlike weapon, often curved

Due bill—A written acknowledgment of indebtedness

Dutch courage—Temporary courage inspired by an intoxicating drink, also the drink itself

Fathom—A unit for measuring depth at sea, equal to two yards

Fill away—To trim the sails so that the wind will catch them full

Forecastle—A short deck in the forepart of a ship

Foremast—The mast nearest to the bow of a ship

Furl—To fold or tie up a sail while leaving it bent so that it catches as little wind as possible

Gaff—A spar for spreading the head of a fore-and-aft sail

Girdling—Mooring with taut cables to prevent swinging by wind or tide

Grog—A mixture of water and spirits, especially rum, first rationed to English sailors in the eighteenth century

Gun-deck—A deck carrying the principal battery of a warship

Gunwale—The upper railing of a ship's side

Halyards—Tackles or ropes to hoist up the sails

Happahs—The modern spelling of this tribe is Hapa'a.

Harpoon—A barbed missile weapon, carrying a long cord, for striking whales

Hatchway—A square hole in a deck, communicating with the hold or another deck

Haul—To shift the course of a ship so as to sail nearer the wind

Hawser—A small cable

Headrails—Rails at the bow of a ship

Heave to—To maneuver a ship into a stationary position so that the sails counteract one another. Also, to lie, in bad weather, keeping the weather bow to the sea.

Helm—Wooden bar through the head of a rudder, a tiller

Hold—The lower compartment of a ship, where provisions are stored

Hove about—The past tense of heave about, to change direction

Howitzer—A piece of artillery

Hull—The body of a ship. When a ship is so far off that you can only see her masts, she is hull down.

Indiaman—A large merchant ship in the India trade

Jack—An iron crosstree at the topgallant masthead

Jib—The foremost sail of a ship, set on a boom that runs out upon the bowsprit

Jolly boat—A small boat

Kedge—A small anchor with an iron stock

Kelp—Any large, coarse seaweed

Lanyards—Short, small ropes to make fast the shrouds and stays

Larboard—The left side

League—A measure of distance. A marine league is about three miles.

Lee—That part of the hemisphere to which the wind is directed

Leeward—Away from the wind

Letter of marque—A document licensing an individual to arm a ship and prey upon enemy merchant shipping. The term is also used to refer to the ships themselves.

Line—A rope

Log—A device, for showing the speed of a ship, consisting of a triangular board (the log chip) weighted on one edge and attached to a line (the log line) that runs out from a reel (the log reel) on shipboard

Magazine—A storeroom for gunpowder and shells aboard ship

Mainmast—The central, and tallest, mast of a ship

Mainsail—A sail carried on the mainmast

Main-topgallant mast—The mast next above the main-topmast on a square-rigged vessel

Main-topmast—The mast next above the mainmast

Manes—Ancestral spirits worshiped as gods

Man-of-war—A naval vessel armed for active hostilities

Mast—The upright timber on which the yards and sails are set.

Master-at-arms—A petty officer who maintains discipline on a ship

Matti—Decoction of an herb, sweetened with sugar and sucked through a tube in Chili. The modern spelling is maté.

Merchantman—A trading vessel

Mess—A number of persons who habitually take their meals together on a ship, or the meal itself

Mizzenmast—The mast that stands nearest to the stern of a ship

Muster—To assemble

Offing—Out to sea, away from the land

Otaheitan—The modern spelling is Tahitian

Packet—A ship for conveying mail, passengers, or cargo

Pay off—To make a ship's head turn away from the direction in which the wind is blowing

Pinnace—A small boat carried by a ship of war for use as a scout or tender

Pipe up—To call to order by means of a boatswain's pipe

Plantain—The fruit of a tropical plant, a type of banana, similar, when cooked, to a potato

Press of sail—All the sail that a ship can set or carry

Privateer—A ship owned and officered by private persons but carrying on maritime war under letters of marque

Purser—A naval paymaster

Quarter—The part of a ship's side between the main chains and the stern

Quartermaster—An officer who assists the navigator

Quoits—A game played by pitching disks at a short stake

Reef—To reduce a sail by tying it, at certain points, around the yard

Reeve—To put a rope through a block

Rigging—All the ropes connected with the masts, spars, and sails

Ropewalk—An alley used for the spinning of rope yarn

Royal mast—The section of a mast next above the topgallant mast

Schooner—A fore-and-aft-rigged vessel originally having two masts

Scurvy—A disease caused by lack of vitamin C in the diet

Seine—Any long fishnet with floats at top edge and weights at bottom

Sheet—A rope fastened to one or both ends of the lower corners of a sail in order to let it out or haul it in

Shoal—A shallow place in a body of water

Skysail—A light sail above the royal mast in a square-rigged ship

Sloop of war—A vessel rigged as either a ship, brig, or schooner and mounting between ten and thirty-two guns

Slops—Articles of clothing sold to sailors on shipboard

Slush from the cask—The greasy refuse of cooking from a ship's galley

Spanker—A fore-and-aft sail extended by a boom and a gaff from the mizzenmast

Spar—A round timber for extending a sail, as a mast or boom

Spermaceti—A white, waxy substance that separates from the oil obtained from the sperm whale

Spring on a cable—A rope made fast to the cable at the bow and taken in at the stern in order to expose the ship's side to any direction

Spritsail—A sail rigged on a spritpole, extending diagonally from the mast

Starboard—The right side

Stays—Large ropes coming from the mastheads down before the masts

Staysail—A sail extended on a stay

Steerage—In a warship, the portion of the berth-deck just forward of the wardroom, the quarters of junior officers

Stern—The after, or rear, end of a ship

Stretch—To stand on different tacks under a press of sail

Studding sails—Light auxiliary sails set out beyond a principal sail by extensible booms during a following wind

Sympathetic ink—A fluid that, when subjected to certain treatment, undergoes a chemical reaction and either changes its color, appears, or vanishes. Of little practical value except for secret correspondence

Tack—To turn a ship against the wind by use of the sails and rudder

Tayees—The modern spelling of the name of the natives of the Taiohae Valley on Nuku Hiva is Te'i'i.

Tippoo Sahib—Sultan of Mysore, killed while besieged by the British in the fortress of Seringapatam in 1799

Top—A platform, surrounding the lower mastheads, to spread the topmast rigging

Topsail—A square sail set next above the lowest sail of a mast

Typees—The modern spelling of the name of the tribe who settled the Taipi Valley on Nuku Hiva is Taipi.

Wardroom—On a warship, the room allotted to the higher-commissioned officers

Watch—A division of a ship's company who keep the deck for an allotted time

Weather a ship—To get to windward of a ship

Windward—Toward that point from which the wind blows

Wind sail—A wide tube or funnel of canvas, used to convey air for ventilation into the lower compartments of a ship

Yardarm—The end of a yard, especially of the yard of a square sail

Yards—The spars upon which the sails are spread

Yeoman—A petty officer who performs clerical duties

Date Due

MAY 26.1972			
OCT. 25.1974			
JAN 32/20			